"The Gestalt Approach
&
Eye Witness to Therapy

is the most concise and at the same time the most profound piece of Gestalt literature I have ever seen. Fritz gives new depth to his philosophy and theory. The transcripts provide excellent illustrations of his techniques."

—*Stella Resnick, Ph.D.,*
Gestalt Institute of
San Francisco

The Gestalt Approach
&
Eye Witness to Therapy

FRITZ PERLS, M.D., Ph.D.

BANTAM BOOKS • TORONTO • NEW YORK • LONDON

This low-priced Bantam Book has been completely reset in a type face designed for easy reading, and was printed from new plates. It contains the complete text of the original hard-cover edition.
NOT ONE WORD HAS BEEN OMITTED.

THE GESTALT APPROACH & EYE WITNESS TO THERAPY
A Bantam Book / published by arrangement with Science and Behavior Books, Inc.

PRINTING HISTORY
Science and Behavior Books edition published May 1973
2nd printing .... November 1973
3rd printing .... August 1974
4th printing .... December 1974
5th printing .... August 1975
Bantam edition / January 1976
2nd printing ..... May 1976
3rd printing .... March 1978
4th printing ... January 1980
5th printing .... August 1981

Photograph of the author on back cover by Deke Simon

The publisher gratefully acknowledges permission granted by Aquarian Productions, Ltd. for the use of transcripts based on their film productions as text in this book. Aquarian Productions, Ltd., 13 Lonsdale Avenue, North Vancouver, B.C., is distributed by Films Incorporated, 1144 Wilmette Avenue, Wilmette, Illinois 60091 (U.S.A.) and by the Visual Education Centre, 95 Berkeley Street, Toronto 2a, Ontario (Canada) and worldwide.

For information address: Science and Behavior Books, Inc. Box 11457, Palo Alto, California 94306

ISBN 0-553-20540-4

Published simultaneously in the United States and Canada

Bantam Books are published by Bantam Books, Inc. Its trademark, consisting of the words "Bantam Books" and the portrayal of a rooster, is Registered in U.S. Patent and Trademark Office and in other countries. Marca Registrada. Bantam Books, Inc., 666 Fifth Avenue, New York, New York 10103.

PRINTED IN THE UNITED STATES OF AMERICA

TABLE OF CONTENTS

PART 2 | EYE WITNESS TO THERAPY

FOREWORD

The Gestalt Approach and *Eye Witness to Therapy* can be read together as one entity and also as two separate works. Fritz Perls was working on both books at the time of his death and had both concepts in mind. I think he would have liked the economy of this presentation.

The Gestalt Approach undoubtedly will become a basic work in gestalt literature. I think Fritz succeeded remarkably well in the task he set for himself. "Any reasonable approach to psychology not hiding behind a professional jargon must be comprehensible to the intelligent layman and must be grounded in the facts of human behavior." Fritz wrote *The Gestalt Approach* because he was no longer satisfied with his two previous theoretical works. Both *Ego, Hunger and Aggression* (1947) and *Gestalt Therapy* (1952) are difficult to read and both are outdated. Fritz had integrated a great deal in the intervening twenty years from many sources; particularly Eastern religions, meditation, psychedelics and body work. Most important, he had lived, loved, fought and practiced for two more decades. Fritz was unique. He was not limited by the role of physician, enemy, charismatic gadfly, lover, dirty old man, artist or writer. He did not age as we usually think of it in the West. Instead age brought increased ability to live in the now and virtuosity in the arts he practiced.

Fritz wrote most of *The Gestalt Approach* in the 1950s, before residing at Esalen during the 1960s. He continued to work on it at Cowichan where he moved in May of 1969. Cowichan is a small lumber town on an inland lake fifty miles north of Victoria on Vancouver Island, British Columbia. Fritz wanted to develop a gestalt community there. I think he had little preconception of the exact form it would take. He hoped a life style would emerge which would encourage increased awareness, with each person integrating disowned parts of his personality and taking responsibility for his own state of consciousness. He wanted a center where therapists could live and study for several months.

I was in Cowichan the last two months that Fritz was there. Fritz said he had never been happier. He evolved a steady mellow pace blending teaching, therapy, play, loving and writing as the need emerged. Fritz became increasingly concerned that many therapists were copying his techniques with limited understanding of his overall theory. He wanted to develop teaching materials that would pull together his personal philosophy and his theory and practice of psychotherapy into a concise exciting form. He asked me to publish *Eye Witness to Therapy.* It would utilize theory from *The Gestalt Approach,* transcripts of his films and transcripts of his lectures at Cowichan. Fritz entrusted these materials to me before leaving Cowichan in early December, 1969. He was to return in the spring to complete this work. Fritz died that winter. I have asked Richard Bandler to undertake editing these materials.

The Gestalt Approach can be read by itself. It also serves as an introduction to *Eye Witness to Therapy.* Richard Bandler has chosen films that are chiefly self-explanatory introductory gestalt work. Several transcripts are included that contain more advanced gestalt work and are representative of transcripts that will appear in later volumes.

A second volume, *Legacy From Fritz* completes the task that Fritz assigned to me. It contains Fritz' lectures at Cowichan. These lectures are informal, sometimes very moving, and show the influence of Eastern philosophy. They are interwoven with unpublished transcripts of tapes and films of advanced gestalt work. Fritz liked these films and recommended intensive study of the films with the transcripts.

A major part of the volume entitled *Gifts from Cowichan* is written by Patricia Baumgardner. She describes her work with Fritz during his last three months of teaching, and how she has integrated these teachings in her clinical practice.

Robert S. Spitzer, M.D.
Editor-in-Chief
Science and Behavior Books

INTRODUCTION

Modern man lives in a state of low-grade vitality. Though generally he does not suffer deeply, he also knows little of true creative living. Instead of it, he has become an anxious automaton. His world offers him vast opportunities for enrichment and enjoyment, and yet he wanders around aimlessly, not really knowing what he wants and completely unable, therefore, to figure out how to get it. He does not approach the adventure of living with either excitement or zest. He seems to feel that the time for fun, for pleasure, for growing and learning, is childhood and youth, and he abdicates life itself when he reaches "maturity." He goes through a lot of motions, but the expression on his face indicates his lack of any real interest in what he is doing. He is usually either poker-faced, bored, aloof, or irritated. He seems to have lost all spontaneity, all capacity to feel and express directly and creatively. He is very good at talking about his troubles and very bad at coping with them. He has reduced life itself to a series of verbal and intellectual exercises; he is drowning himself in a sea of words. He has substituted psychiatric and pseudo-psychiatric explanations of life for the process of living. He spends endless time trying either to recapture the past or to mold the future. His present activities are merely bothersome chores he has to get out of the way. At times, he is not even aware of his actions at the moment.

All this may seem a sweeping statement, but the time has come when such a statement needs to be made. The last fifty years have seen an enormous growth in man's understanding of himself. They have seen an enormous growth in our understanding of the mechanisms—both physiological and psychological—by which we maintain ourselves under the constantly changing pressures and conditions of life. But they have seen no corresponding increase in our capacity to enjoy ourselves; to use our knowledge for our own interests; to expand and widen our sense of aliveness and growth. Understanding human behavior for the sake of understanding it is a pleasant intellectual game, an amusing or tortured way of whiling away time, but it has no necessary relationship to or usefulness in the daily business of living. As a matter of fact, much of our neurotic dissatisfaction with ourselves and our world stems from the fact that, while we have swallowed whole many of the terms and concepts of modern psychiatry and psychology, we have not digested them, tested them, or used our verbal and intellectual knowledge as the tool of power it is supposed to be. On the contrary, many of us use psychiatric concepts as rationalizations, as ways of perpetuating unsatisfactory present behavior. We justify our current unhappiness by our past experiences, and wallow in our misery. We use our knowledge of man as an excuse for socially destructive and self-destructive behavior. We have graduated from the infant's "I can't help myself," to the adult's "I can't help myself because . . . my mother rejected me when I was a child; because I never learned to appreciate my Oedipus complex; because I'm too introverted." But psychiatry and psychology were never meant to be after-the-fact justifications for continuing neurotic behavior, behavior which does not permit the individual to live up to the maximum of his capacities. The aim of these sciences is not merely to offer explanations of behavior, it is to help us arrive at *self-knowledge, satisfaction and self-support*.

Perhaps one of the reasons psychiatry in particular has lent itself to this perversion is that too many of the classical theories of psychiatry have been petrified, by their proponents, into dogma. In the effort to fit all the different shapes and sizes of human behavior into the Procrustes' bed of theory, many psychiatric schools either ignore or condemn those aspects of man's ways of living which stubbornly resist explanation in terms of their own pet arguments. Instead of abandoning or changing a theory when it no longer adequately conforms with the facts, and when it no longer adequately serves to solve difficulties, they twist the facts of behavior to suit the theory. This serves neither to increase understanding nor to help man solve his problems.

This book is an explanation of a somewhat new approach to the entire subject of human behavior—both in its actuality and its potentiality. It is written from the belief that man can live a fuller, richer life than most of us now do. It is written from the conviction that man has not yet even begun to discover the potential of energy and enthusiasm that lies in him. The book endeavors to bring together a theory and a practical application of that theory to the problems of daily life and to the techniques of psychotherapy. The theory itself is grounded in experience and observation; it has grown and changed with years of practice and application, *and it is still growing.*

PART I | THE GESTALT APPROACH

1 | FOUNDATIONS

Gestalt Psychology

Any reasonable approach to psychology not hiding itself behind a professional jargon must be comprehensible to the intelligent layman, and must be grounded in the facts of human behavior. If it is not, there is something basically wrong with it. Psychology deals, after all, with the one subject of most interest to human beings—ourselves and others. The understanding of psychology, and of ourselves, must be consistent. If we cannot understand ourselves, we can never hope to understand what we are doing, we can never hope to solve our problems, we can never hope to live rewarding lives. However, such understanding of the 'self' involves more than the usual intellectual understanding. It requires feeling and sensitivity too.

The approach here presented rests on a set of premises that are neither abstruse nor unreasonable. On the contrary, they are, by and large, common sense assumptions which experience can easily verify. As a matter of fact, although they are frequently expressed in complicated terminology which serves the triple function of confusing the reader, inflating the self-importance of the writer and obscuring the issues they are meant to enlighten, these assumptions underlie a large part of contemporary psychology. Unfortunately, too many psychologists take them for granted and push them into the background, while their theory gallops further and further away from reality and the observable. But if we bring these premises, simply expressed, out into the open, we will be able to use them continually as a yardstick against which to measure the reliability and the utility of our concepts, and we will be able to undertake our exploration with both pleasure and profit.

Let us introduce the first premise through an illustration. We said earlier that the approach outlined in this book is in many ways new. This does not mean that this approach has no relationship to any other theory of human behavior or to any other applications of theory to the problems of daily life or psychotherapeutic practice. Nor does it mean that this approach is composed exclusively of new and revolutionary elements. Most of the elements in it are to be found in many other approaches to the subject. What is new here is not necessarily the individual bits and pieces that go to make up the theory, *rather it is the way they are used and organized which gives this approach its uniqueness and its claim on your attention.* The first basic premise of this book is implicit in that last sentence. The premise is that it is the organization of facts, perceptions, behavior or phenomena, and not the individual items of which they are composed, that defines them and gives them their specific and particular meaning.

Originally, this concept was developed by a group of German psychologists working in the field of perception, who showed that man does not perceive things as unrelated isolates, but organizes them in the perceptual process into meaningful wholes. A man coming into a room full of people, for example, does not perceive merely blobs of color and movement, faces and bodies. He perceives the room and the people in it as a unit, in which one element, selected from the many present, stands out, while the others recede into the background. The choice of which element will stand out is made as a result of many factors, all of which can be lumped together under the general term *interest.* As long as there is interest, the whole scene will appear to be organized in a meaningful way. It is only when interest is completely lacking that perception is atomized, and the room is seen as a jumble of unrelated objects.

Let us see how this principle operates in a simple

situation. Suppose that the room is a living room, and the occasion is a cocktail party. Most of the guests are already present; the latecomers are gradually dribbling in. A new arrival enters. He is a chronic alcoholic, and he wants a drink desperately. To him, the other guests, the chairs and couches, the pictures on the walls—all will be unimportant and will recede into the background. He will make straight for the bar; of all the objects in the room, that one will be foreground to him. Now another guest comes in. She is a painter, and the hostess has just purchased one of her works. Her primary concern is to find out how and where her picture is hanging. She will select the painting from all the other objects in the room. Like the alcoholic, she will be completely unconcerned with the people, and will head for her work like a homing pigeon. Or take the case of the young man who has come to the party to meet his current girl friend. He will scan the crowd, will search among the faces of the guests until he finds her. She will be foreground, everything else background. For that peripatetic guest who flits from group to group, from conversation to conversation, from bar to couch, from hostess to cigarette box, the room will appear to be patterned differently at different times. While he is talking with one group, that group and that conversation will be foreground. When, towards the end of his chat, he feels tired and decides to sit down, the one vacant seat on the sofa will be foreground. As his interests shifts, his perception of the room, the people and objects in it, and even himself, changes. Foreground and background are interchanged, they do not remain static as they do, for example, to the young swain, whose interest is fixed and invariable. Now comes our last guest. He, like so many of us at cocktail parties, didn't want to come in the first place and has no real interest in the entire proceedings. For him the entire scene will remain disorganized and meaningless unless and until something happens to make him focus his interest and attention.

The school of psychology which developed out of these observations is called the Gestalt School. Gestalt is a German word for which there is no exact English equivalent. A gestalt is a pattern, a configuration, the particular form of organization of the individual parts that go into its make up. The basic premise of Gestalt psychology is that human nature is organized into patterns or wholes, that it is experienced by the individual in these terms, and that it can only be understood as a function of the patterns or wholes of which it is made.

Homeostasis

Our next premise is that all life and all behavior are governed by the process which scientists call homeostasis, and which the layman calls adaptation. The homeostatic process is the process by which the organism maintains its equilibrium and therefore its health under varying conditions. Homeostasis is thus the process by which the organism satisfies its needs. Since its needs are many, and each need upsets the equilibrium, the homeostatic process goes on all the time. All life is characterized by this continuing play of balance and imbalance in the organism. When the homeostatic process fails to some degree, when the organism remains in a state of disequilibrium for too long a time and is unable to satisfy its needs, it is sick. When the homeostatic process fails, the organism dies.

A few simple examples will serve to make this clear. The human body functions efficiently only when the level of sugar in the blood is kept within certain limits. If the blood sugar content falls below these limits, the adrenal glands secrete adrenalin; the adrenalin makes the liver turn its stores of glycogen into sugar; this sugar passes into the blood and brings the blood sugar up. All of this occurs on a purely physiological basis; the organism is not aware of what is happening. But a drop in the blood sugar level has still another effect. It is accompanied by the sensation of hunger, and the organism satisfies its dissatisfaction and disequilibrium by eating. The food is digested, a certain amount of it becomes sugar, and the sugar is restored to the blood. Thus, in the case of eating, the homeostatic process demands awareness and some deliberate action on the part of the organism.

When the blood sugar rises excessively, the pancreas secretes more insulin, and this causes the liver to remove sugar from the blood. The kidneys also help to remove this excess; sugar is excreted into the urine. These processes, like the first ones we described, are purely physiological. But the blood sugar content can be lowered deliberately, as the result of an act of awareness. The medical term for that chronic failure of homeostasis which results in a constant excess of blood sugar is diabetes. The diabetic's system apparently cannot control itself. However, the patient can supply a control by artificially adding insulin through injection. This reduces the blood sugar content to the proper level.

Let us take another example. For the organism to be in good health, the water content of the blood must also be kept at a certain level. When it drops below that level, sweating, salivation and the excretion of urine are all diminished, and the body tissues pass some of their water into the blood stream. So the body sees to it that it conserves water during such an emergency period. This is the physiological side of the process. But when the water content of the blood drops too low, the individual feels thirst. He then does what he can to maintain the necessary balance. He takes a drink of water. When the water content of the blood is excessive, all these activities are reversed, just as they are in the case of the blood sugar. Even more simply we could say this: The physiological term for loss of water in the blood is dehydration; chemically it can be expressed as the loss of a certain number of units of H_2O; sensorially it is felt as thirst, with its symptoms of mouth dryness and restlessness; and psychologically it is felt as the wish to drink.

Thus we might call the homeostatic process the process of *self-regulation,* the process by which the organism interacts with its environment. Although the examples I have given here involve complex activity on the part of the organism, they both deal with the simplest and most elemental functions, all of which operate in the service of survival for the individual and, through him, of the species. The need to maintain the level of blood sugar and water within certain limits is basic to all animal life. But there are other needs, not so closely related to questions of life and death, in which the process of homeostasis also functions. The human being can see better with two eyes than with one; but if one eye is destroyed, the victim is able to continue living. He is no longer a two-eyed organism. He is a one-eyed organism and he soon learns to function efficiently within this situation, to gauge what his new needs are and to find the adaptive means for satisfying them.

The organism has psychological *contact* needs as well as physiological ones; these are felt every time the psychological equilibrium is disturbed, just as the physiological needs are felt every time the physiological equilibrium is disturbed. These psychological needs are met through what we might call the psychological counterpart of the homeostatic process. Let me make it very clear, however, that this psychological process cannot be divorced from the physiological one; that each contains elements of the other. Those needs that are primarily psychological in nature and the homeostatic or adaptive mechanisms by which they are met constitute part of the subject matter of psychology.

Human beings have thousands of such needs on the purely physiological level. And on the social levels, there are other thousands of needs. The more intensely they are felt to be essential to continued life, the more closely we identify ourselves with them, the more intensely we will direct our activities towards satisfying them.

Here again, the static concepts of the older psychologies have stood in the way of understanding. Noting certain common drives among all living creatures, the theoreticians postulated the "instincts" as the guiding forces in life, and described neurosis as the result of the repression of those instincts. MacDougall's list of instincts included fourteen. Freud considered the two basic and most important to be Eros (sex or life) and Thanatos (death). But if we could classify all the disturbances of the organismic balance, we would find thousands of instincts, and these would differ among themselves in intensity.

There is still another weakness in this theory. We can agree, I think, that the need to survive acts as a compelling force in all living creatures and that all show, at all times, two important tendencies: to survive, as individuals and as species, and to grow. These are fixed goals. But the ways in which they are met vary, from situation to situation, from species to species, from individual to individual. If a nation's survival is threatened by war, its citizens will take up arms. If an individual's survival is threatened because his blood sugar level is too low, he will look for food. Scheherezade's survival was threatened by the Sultan, and to meet the threat she told him stories for a thousand and one nights. Shall we then say that she had a story telling instinct?

The whole instinct theory tends to confuse needs with their symptoms, or with the means we use to achieve them. And it is from this confusion that the conception of the repression of instincts arose.

For the instincts (if they exist) cannot be repressed. They are out of reach of our awareness, and thus out of reach of our deliberate action. We cannot repress the need to survive, for example, but we can and do interfere with its symptoms and signs. This is done by interrupting the ongoing process, by preventing ourselves from carrying out whatever action is appropriate.

But what happens if several needs (or instincts, if you prefer) come into existence simultaneously? The healthy organism seems to operate within what we might call a hierarchy of values. Since it is unable to do more than one thing properly at a time, it attends to the dominant survival need before it attends to any of the others; it operates on the principle of first things first. Once in Africa I observed a group of deer grazing within a hundred yards of a pack of sleeping lions. When one of the lions awoke and began to roar in hunger, the deer took speedy flight. Now try for a moment to imagine yourself in the deer's place. Suppose you were running for your life. Soon you would run out of breath, then you would have to slow down or stop altogether until you got a second wind. At that point, breathing would have become a greater emergency—a greater need—than running, just as running had previously become a greater need than eating.

Formulating this principle in terms of Gestalt psychology, we can say that the dominant need of the organism, at any time, becomes the foreground figure, and the other needs recede, at least temporarily, into the background. The foreground is that need which presses most sharply for satisfaction, whether the need is, as in our example, the need to preserve life itself, or whether it is related to less physically vital areas—whether it is physiological or psychological. It seems to be a need of mothers, for example, to keep their infants happy and contented; discomfort in the child produces discomfort in them. The mother of a young baby may be able to sleep soundly through the noises of rumbling trucks or even through crashing, deafening peals of thunder, but she will waken in an instant if her baby—in another room at the end of a long hall—so much as whimpers.

For the individual to satisfy his needs, to close the gestalt, to move on to other business, he must be able to sense what he needs and he must know how to manipulate himself and his environment, for even the purely physiological needs can only be satisfied through the interaction of the organism and the environment.

The Holistic Doctrine

One of the most observable facts about man is that he is a unified organism. And yet this fact is completely ignored by the traditional schools of psychiatry and psychotherapy which, no matter how they describe their approach, are still operating in terms of the old mind-body split. Since the emergence of psychosomatic medicine, the close relationship between mental and physical activity has become increasingly apparent. And yet, because of the persistence of psycho-physical parallelism, even this advance in understanding has not achieved as much as it should. It is still tied to the concepts of causality, treating functional disease as a physical disturbance caused by a psychic event.

What seems to have happened in the development of psychological thinking is as follows. We observe that man is able to function on two qualitatively different levels: the level of thinking and the level of acting. We are struck by the differences between the two and by their apparent independence from one another. And so we postulate that they are different orders of matter. Then we are compelled to postulate the existence of some as yet undiscovered structural entity, the mind, which is described as the seat of mental activity. Since the development of depth psychology, springing out of the observation that man is not purely a rational creature, the mind, which previously had been considered exclusively as the font of reason, now becomes also the seat of the murky unconscious and a structure which is capable of exercising its will, not only over the body, but also over itself. Thus, the mind can repress thoughts and memories it finds offensive. It can convert symptoms from one area of the body to another. It is the little deus ex machina which controls us in every respect.

Because the quantitative analysis of physiological processes progressed so much more rapidly than the quantitative analysis of mental processes, we also tended to accept considerably more as given about the body than about the mind. We do not quarrel with the scientific facts of physiology and anatomy. We can describe the heart, the liver, the muscular and circulatory systems, and we know how they operate. We recognize that the ability to perform certain physical and physiological activities is built into man, and we have lost our sense of wonder at our marvelous efficiency. We know, too, a great deal about the brain and the way it functions, and we are learning more every day. But until we have gone further in this study, we will still have limited understanding of another one of man's basic built-in capacities: the ability to learn and manipulate symbols and abstractions. That ability seems to be associated with the greater development and complexity of his brain. And it is as natural to man as is his ability to clench his fists or walk or have sexual intercourse.

This symbol-using capacity shows itself in what we call mental activity, whether it is directed towards the production of scientific theories or towards the production of a trite statement about the weather. Even what we consider a low order of mental activity requires a great deal of ability to deal with symbols and to combine abstractions. Comparably, even what we consider a low order of physical activity—the state of sleep, for example—requires a considerable use of our built-in physiological capacities. The muscles are not as active during sleep as they are in the waking state, but some degree of activity there inevitably is.

Given, then, that the human being has a built-in ability to use symbols and to abstract (and even the most rigid behaviorist has to admit this; if the ability did not exist he could not conduct an argument about its existence) what is the human being doing when he uses it? He is, I maintain, acting in effigy. He is doing *symbolically* what he could do *physically*. If he thinks about a scientific theory, he could write it down or explain it verbally. Writing and speaking are physical actions. That he can think up scientific theories is truly remarkable—but it is really no more remarkable than the fact that he can write or speak.

Thinking, of course, is not the only mental activity we engage in. The mind has other functions, too.

There is the function of attention. When we say, "I put my mind on a problem," we do not mean that we take some physical body from inside ourselves and deposit it heavily and with a thud on that problem. We mean "I concentrate much of my activity and my sensory perceptions on this problem."

We also talk of awareness, which could be described as the fuzzy twin of attention. Awareness is more diffuse than attention—it implies a relaxed rather than a tense perception by the whole person.

And we talk of will. Here the area of attention or

awareness is highly limited in scope, and the person focuses on initiating and carrying through a certain set of actions directed towards certain specific goals.

In all of these mental activities, the relationship between what we do and what we think is very clear. When we are aware of something, or focus attention on it, or attempt to exert our will on it, there are at least some overt signs by which the spectator can see that these processes are at work. The man who is concentrating hard on understanding what someone else is saying is likely to be sitting forward in his chair; his whole being seems to be aimed and directed towards that in which he is interested. The man who makes up his mind not to take that fifth piece of candy is likely to make a motion towards it, and to stop his hand suddenly and withdraw it before it reaches the candy dish.

But let me return to the area of thinking. It is here that most of the confusion arises. We understand thinking to include a number of activities—dreaming, imagining, theorizing, anticipating—making maximum use of our capacity to manipulate symbols. For the sake of brevity, let us call all of this *fantasy* activity rather than thinking. We tend to attach the notion of reason to thinking and of unreason to dreaming, and yet the two activities are very much alike. Let me make it very clear, however, that I do not mean, by using the word fantasy, to imply that there is anything unreal, eerie, strange, or false about these activities. Fantasy activity, in the broad sense in which I am using the term, is that activity of the human being which through the use of symbols tends to reproduce reality on a diminished scale. As activity involving the use of symbols, it derives from reality, since symbols themselves are initially derived from reality. Symbols begin as labels for objects and processes; they proliferate and grow into labels for labels and labels for labels for labels. The symbols may not even be approximated in reality, but they start in reality.

The same thing is true of fantasy activity, which is internal symbol-using activity. Here the reality reproduction may stray far from its origins, from the reality with which it was originally connected. But it is in some way always related to a reality which has a meaningful existence for the person into whose fantasy activity it enters. I do not see a real tree in my mind's eye, but the correspondence between the real tree in my garden and my fantasy tree is sufficient to make it possible for me to connect one with the other. When I mull over a problem, trying to determine which course of action I will take in a given situation, it is as if I were doing two very real things. Firstly, I have a conversation about my problem—in reality I might have this conversation with a friend. Secondly, I reproduce in my mind's eye the situation into which my decision will precipitate me. I anticipate in fantasy what will happen in reality, and although the correspondence between my fantasy anticipation and the actual situation may not be absolute, just as the correspondence between the tree in my mind's eye and the tree in my garden is not absolute, just as the correspondence between the word "tree" and the object tree is only approximate, it is close enough for me to base my actions upon it.

Thus mental activity seems to act as a time, energy, and work saver for the individual. The lever, for example, works on the principle that a small force applied at one end of the instrument produces a large force at the other. If I put one end of a lever under a five-hundred pound rock and bear down heavily on the other end of the tool, I can move an object so heavy that it would otherwise resist all my attempts to change its position.

When I fantasize, or put my attention on a problem, I use a small amount of my available energy internally in order to produce a larger amount of efficiently distributed body or external energy. We think about problems in fantasy in order to be able to solve them in reality. Instead of simply going to the supermarket with absolutely no idea of what she will purchase, the housewife decides beforehand what she needs and she is thus able to act more efficiently once she gets to the store. She does not have to rush from display case to display case, deciding at each step of the way whether or not she needs the particular item available for purchase. She saves time, energy, and activity.

Now we are ready to formulate a definition of the functions of the mind and a definition of mental activity as a part of the whole organism we call the human being. Mental activity seems to be activity of the whole person carried on at a lower energy level than those activities we call physical. Here I must stop to point out that by using the word "lower" I am implying no value judgment at all. I simply mean that the activities we call mental require less expenditure of the body substance than do those we call physical. All of us take it for granted that the sedentary professor can get along on fewer calories than the ditch-digger. As water changes to steam by the application of heat, so covert body activity changes to the latent, private activity we call mental by a diminution of intensity. And conversely, as steam turns into water by the application of cold, so the latent, private activity we call mental changes into overt body activity by an increase of intensity. The organism acts with and reacts to its environment with greater or lesser intensity; as the intensity diminishes, physical behavior turns into mental behavior. As the intensity increases, mental behavior turns into physical behavior.

One further example should serve to make this concept entirely clear. When a man is actually attacking an enemy, he shows enormous overt body activity. He contracts his muscles, his heart beats faster, adrenalin is poured into his blood stream in large quantities, his breathing becomes rapid and shallow, his jaws are clenched and rigid, his whole body becomes tense. When he talks about how much he dislikes this enemy he will still show a large number of overt physical signs, although there will be fewer of these than when he is actually fighting. When he feels anger, and thinks about attacking an enemy, he still shows some overt physical signs. But these signs are less visible and less intense than they were when he was actually fighting, or when he was talking about it. His behavior is now of still lower intensity. His overt physical activity has changed to covert mental activity.

Our capacity to act on a level of diminished intensity —to engage in mental behavior—is of tremendous advantage not only for the individual human being in solving his own particular problems, but for the entire species. The energy man saves by thinking things out instead of acting them out in every situation can now be invested in enriching his life. He can make and use tools which further save him energy and therefore offer him even greater opportunities for enrichment. But these are not the only advantages. Man's ability to abstract and to combine abstractions, his capacity to invent symbols, to create art and science—all these are intimately connected with his ability to fantasize. The basic ability to create and use symbols is enhanced by the real products of symbol using. Each generation inherits the fantasies of all preceding generations, and thus accumulates greater knowledge and understanding.

This conception of human life and behavior as made up of levels of activity does away once and for all with the disturbing and unsatisfying psycho-physical parallelism with which psychology has been coping ever since its birth. It enables us to see the mental and physical sides of human behavior not as independent entities which could have their existence apart from human beings or from one another, which was the inevitable and logical conclusion to the older psychologies, but to look at the human being as he is, as a whole, and to examine his behavior as it manifests itself on the overt level of physical activity and the covert level of mental activity. Once we recognize that thoughts and actions are made of the same stuff, we can translate and transpose from one level to another.

Thus we can introduce finally into psychology a holistic concept—the concept of the unified field—which scientists have always longed to find and towards which the contemporary psychosomaticists have been groping.

In psychotherapy, this concept gives us a tool for dealing with the whole man. Now we can see how his mental and physical actions are meshed together. We can observe man more keenly and use our observations more meaningfully. For how much broader now is the surface which we can observe! If mental and physical activity are of the same order, we can observe both as manifestations of the same thing: man's being. Neither patient nor therapist is limited by what the patient says and thinks, both can now take into consideration what he *does*. What he does provides clues as to what he thinks, as what he thinks provides clues as to what he does, and what he would like to do. Between the levels of thinking and doing there is an intermediate stage, the stage of playing at, and in therapy, if we observe keenly, we will notice that the patient plays at a lot of things. He himself will know what his actions, his fantasies and his play-actings mean, if we but call them to his attention. He himself will provide his own interpretations.

Through his experience of himself on the three levels of fantisizing, play-acting, and doing, he will come to an understanding of himself. Psychotherapy then becomes not an excavation of the past, in terms of repressions, Oedipal conflicts, and primal scenes, but an experience in living in the present. In this living situation, the patient learns for himself how to intergrate his thoughts, feelings, and actions not only while he is in the consulting room, but during the course of his everyday life. The neurotic obviously does not feel like a whole person. He feels as if his conflicts and unfinished business were tearing him to shreds. But with his recognition that he is, being human, a whole, comes the ability to regain that sense of wholeness which is his birthright.

Contact Boundary

No individual is self-sufficient; the individual can exist only in an environmental field. The individual is inevitably, at every moment, a part of some field. His behavior is a function of the total field, which includes both him and his environment. The nature of the relationship between him and his environment determines the human being's behavior. If the relationship is mutually satisfactory, the individual's behavior is what we call normal. If the relationship is one of conflict, the individual's behavior is described as abnormal. The environment does not create the individual, nor does the individual create the environment. Each is what it is, each has its own particular character, because of its relationship to the other and the whole. The study of the human organism alone, of what goes on entirely inside him, is the province of anatomy and physiology. The study of the environment alone, of what goes on entirely outside him, is the province of the physical, geographical and social sciences. In these sciences, elements of the total field—which includes both the individual and the environment—can be abstracted and studied alone because the concern of these fields is precisely with those elements which exist independently of one another. The structure of the human eye has no influence on the structure of the objects it sees. Nor does the structure of these objects affect the structure of the eye. But psychology cannot make such abstractions, nor can it deal with structure per se. The study of the way the human being functions in his environment is the study of what goes on at the contact boundary between the individual and his environment. It is at this contact boundary that the psychological events take place. Our thoughts, our actions, our behavior, and our emotions are our way of experiencing and meeting these boundary events.

With this concept we come to a parting of the ways with the older psychologies. They established another split. Like the mind-body split, they proceeded to treat their postulated abstraction as a factual reality, and then compounded the confusion in their effort to extricate themselves from the mess they had gotten themselves into. They split experience into inside and outside and then were faced with the insoluble question of whether man is ruled by forces from without or from within. This either-or approach, this need for a simple causality, this neglect of the total field, makes problems out of situations which are in reality indivisible.

True enough, I can divide the sentence "I see a tree" into subject, verb, and object. But in experience, the process cannot be split up in this way. There is no sight without something to be seen. Nor is anything seen if there is no eye to see it. Yet by splitting experience into inside and outside in this way, and then dealing with their abstractions—inside and outside—as if they were experiential realities, scientists had to find some explanation of each. And of course, in actuality, neither can be explained without the other.

To explain the inner experience, the theory of the reflex arc was devised: first the stimulus (the outside) reaches the receptor (the sensory organs), then impulses are carried through the intermediate system (the nerves) to the effector (the muscles). True enough, we act through two systems, the sensoric and the motoric. But the organism reaches out towards the world with both. His sensory system provides him with an *orientation*, his motor system with a means of *manipulation*. Neither is a function of the other, neither is temporally or logically prior to the other, they are both functions of the total human being.

With this new outlook, the environment and the organism stand in a relationship of mutuality to one another. Neither is the victim of the other. Their relationship is actually that of dialectical opposites. To satisfy its needs, the organism has to find its required supplements in the environment. The system of orientation discovers what is wanted; all living creatures are observably able to sense what the outside objects are that will satisfy their needs. The hungry puppy is not confused by the myriad of shapes, smells, noises, and colors in the world; he goes directly for his mother's teat. This is the foreground figure.

Once the system of orientation has done its job, the organism has to manipulate the object it needs in such a way that the organismic balance will be restored, the gestalt will be closed. The mother wakened by her crying baby will not be content to lie comfortably back in her bed listening to her offspring wail. She will do something to eliminate the disturbance. She will try to satisfy the baby's needs, and when they are satisfied, she too can return to sleep. The puppy, having found the teat, will suck.

These concepts, too, have meaning in psychotherapy. First of all, the conception that effective action is action directed towards the satisfaction of a dominant need gives us a clue as to the meaning of specific forms of behavior. Secondly, it gives us a further tool for an understanding of neurosis. If, through some disturbance in the homeostatic process, the individual is unable to sense his dominant needs or to manipulate his environment in order to attain them, he will behave in a disorganized and ineffective way. He will be trying to do too many things at once.

You will, I am sure, have noticed in your own experience that if your attention is divided between two objects of interest, you cannot concentrate properly on either. This inability to concentrate is a frequent complaint of the neurotic. When there are more than two objects demanding our attention, or if the object of interest is hazy, we feel confused. If there are two inconsistent situations requiring our attention we speak of conflict. If these are permanent and apparently insoluble, we regard them as neurotic conflicts.

The neurotic has lost the ability (or perhaps he never developed it) to organize his behavior in accordance with a necessary hierarchy of needs. He literally cannot concentrate. In therapy, he has to learn how to distinguish the myriad of needs from one another, and how to attend to them, one at a time. He must learn to discover and identify himself with his needs, he must learn how, at every moment, to become totally involved in what he is doing; how to stick with a situation long enough to close the gestalt and move on to other business. *Organization plus environment equals field.*

Let me return for a moment to the discussion of the organism's relationship to the field, or, in more specific terms, the individual's relationship to his environment. Not only does he have needs and a system of orientation and manipulation with which to achieve their satisfaction, he has attitudes towards those things in the environment that can help or hinder his search for satisfaction. Freud described this by saying that objects in the world receive a cathexis. In Gestalt terms, we would say that these objects become figure. Those that are desirable because they help to satisfy the individual's needs and to restore the disturbed equilibrium are said to have a positive cathexis. Water has a positive cathexis for a thirsty man, a soft bed for a tired man. Those that are undesirable because they threaten the individual or tend to upset his equilibrium, or do not satisfy his needs, have a negative cathexis. For the hunter threatened by a rampaging elephant, the elephant has a negative cathexis.

Man is suspended between *impatience* and *dread*. Each need requires immediate gratification without any lapse of time. Impatience, then, is the emotional form which excitement—produced by the presence of a need and the disturbance of balance—assumes first. Impatience is the basis of positive cathexis. Dread, on the other hand, is the basis of all negative cathexis; it is the anti-survival experience. The dreadful is experienced as vague, undifferentiated danger; as soon as there is an object to cope with, dread diminishes into fear. As the positive cathexis indicates the life supporting supplements, so negative cathexis indicates danger, diminished support, or even death. In any case, it threatens that some or all of our existence is at stake, whether it is the physical being (illness), sexual integrity (castration), self-concept (humiliation), weltanschauung (existential confusion), security (economic depression), or any one of a number of other things.

The individual wants to appropriate or take over those objects or people in the environment which have a positive cathexis; the young man in love wants to marry the girl of his choice, the hungry man wants to eat. In trying to acquire the positively cathexed objects, the individual *contacts* his environment, he reaches out towards it. On the other hand, the individual has an entirely different orientation towards those objects or people that have a negative cathexis. These he wants to annihilate or remove from the field. This applies to our fantasy as well as to the actual world. The farmer will try to shoot the fox that is raiding his chicken coop. We try to remove "bad" thoughts and unwanted emotions from our "minds" as if they were actual enemies.

The safest way to annihilate the enemy is, of course, to destroy him or render him harmless. This means destroying those of his qualities that support his threat against us. When Delilah cut off Sampson's hair, she did just that. The next best thing would be to frighten or threaten him, to chase him out. In addition to these methods of destruction, we can cope with the negatively cathexed situation or object by magic annihilation or by flight from the danger field. Both are means of *withdrawal.*

Magic annihilation is well known in psychotherapy under the name of *scotoma,* that is, blind spot. There are people who literally do not see what they don't want to see, don't hear what they don't want to hear, don't feel what they don't want to feel—all this in order to shut out what they consider to be dangerous—the objects or situations that have a negative cathexis for them. Magic annihilation is a partial withdrawal, a substitute for actual withdrawal.

In this age of psychoanalysis, we tend to think of withdrawal as one of the symptoms of neurosis. But this is a misunderstanding of the phenomenon. Withdrawal per se is neither good nor bad, it is simply a means of coping with danger. The question of whether or not it is pathological can only be answered by our answers to these questions: withdrawal from what, withdrawal to what, and withdrawal for how long?

The same thing applies to contact. Contact itself is neither good nor bad, although in our age of concern for "social adjustment" we tend to value the capacity to make contact almost above all others. Yet some forms of contact are anything but healthy. You yourself must have known people who simply have to stay in continual contact with you: the hangers-on. Every psychotherapist knows that they are as difficult to treat as the deeply withdrawn personalities. There are some people who feel compelled to stay in contact with their fixed ideas; they are as disturbed as the schizophrenics who withdraw almost completely.

Hence, not every contact is healthy and not every withdrawal unhealthy. One of the characteristics of the neurotic is that he can neither make good contact nor can he organize his withdrawal. When he should be in contact with his environment, his mind is somewhere else, and so he cannot concentrate. When he should withdraw, he cannot. Insomnia, a frequent complaint of the neurotic, is an example of the inability to withdraw, the phenomenon of boredom is another. Boredom occurs when we try to stay in contact with a subject that does not hold our interest. We quickly exhaust any excitement at our disposal; we get tired and lean back. We want to withdraw from the situations. If we cannot find a suitable excuse to do so, the over-contact becomes painful, and we express it in exactly these terms. We're "bored to death," or "bored to tears." If we let our tiredness take over, we will withdraw to our fantasy, to a more interesting contact. That our tiredness is really only a temporary matter is apparent from the renewed interest we feel when we suddenly find ourselves leaning forward to listen attentively to a more fascinating speaker. Once again we are in contact—we are "all there."

Contact and withdrawal are dialectical opposites. They are descriptions of the ways we meet psychological events, they are our means of dealing at the contact boundary with objects in the field. In the organism/environment field the positive and negative (contact and withdrawal) cathexis behave very similarly to the attracting and repelling forces of magnetism. As a matter of fact, the whole organism/environment field is one unit which is dialectically differentiated. It is differentiated biologically into the organism and the environment, psychologically into the self and the other, morally into selfishness and altruism, scientifically into subjective and objective, etc.

When the cathected object, whether its cathexis is positive or negative, has been appropriated or annihilated, contacted or withdrawn from, or dealt with in some way satisfactory to the individual, both it and the need with which it is associated disappear from the environment; *the gestalt is closed*. The cathected object and the need have an almost mathematical relationship to one another; if the need is a minus, the cathected object is a plus. If a man is thirsty, he feels a lack of fluid, his need is experienced as a minus in him. At that time a glass of water has a positive cathexis for him, and it is experienced as a plus. The exact number of units of fluid he needs can be measured, and when he gets that number from the environment his needs are satisfied. The sum, as it were, of the need and the cathected object is zero.

This contact with and withdrawal from the environment, this acceptance and rejection of the environment, are the most important functions of the total personality. They are the positive and negative aspects of the psychological processes by which we live. They are dialectical opposites, part of the same thing, the total personality. Those psychologists who maintain a dualistic conception of man see them operating as opposing forces which tear the individual into pieces. We, on the other hand, see them as aspects of the same thing: *the capacity to discriminate*. This capacity can become confused and can function badly. When it does, the individual is unable to behave appropriately and consequently we describe him as a neurotic. But when the capacity to discriminate functions well, the components of acceptance and rejection, of contact and withdrawal, are always present and active.

Indeed, this function seems to be part of the very rhythm of life itself. During the day, when we are awake, we are in touch with the world, we are in contact with it. During the night when we are asleep, we withdraw, we give up contact. In summer we are usually more outgoing than in winter. Wintertime withdrawal is perfectly exemplified by those animals which hibernate, sleeping through the entire season.

Contacting the environment is, in a sense, forming a gestalt. Withdrawing is either closing it completely or rallying one's forces to make closure possible. The prize-fighter makes contact with his opponent's jaw but he does not leave his fist there. He withdraws it for the next blow. If contact is overprolonged, it becomes ineffective or painful; if withdrawal is overprolonged, it interferes with the processes of life. Contact and withdrawal, in a rhythmic pattern, are our means of satisfying our needs, of continuing the ongoing processes of life itself.

Now we have the hierarchy of needs, the equipment —sensory and motor—with which to satisfy them, the positive and negative cathexes of the field, contact and withdrawal, impatience and dread. This brings us to the question of the force which basically energizes all our action. That force seems to be emotion. For although modern psychiatry treats emotions as if they were a bothersome surplus that had to be discharged, emotions are the very life of us. We can theorize and interpret the emotions any way we will. But this is a waste of time. For emotions are the very language of the organism; they modify the basic excitement according to the situation which has to be met. Excitement is transformed into specific emotions, and the emotions are transformed into sensoric and motor actions. The emotions energize the cathexes and mobilize the ways and means of satisfying needs.

Here again are some cues for psychotherapy. Earlier, we described neurosis as the illness which arises when the individual somehow interrupts the ongoing processes of life and saddles himself with so many unfinished situations that he cannot satisfactorily get on with the process of living. The interruptions we described as psychological, or neurotic, were, as contrasted with those that we call physiological, of the kind that take place either on the level of awareness or on a level which can be made aware. We now see something else about the neurotic. His contact-withdrawal rhythm is out of kilter. He cannot decide for himself when to participate and when to withdraw because all the unfinished business of his life, all the interruptions to the ongoing process, have disturbed his sense of orientation, and he is no longer able to distinguish between those objects or persons in the environment which have a positive cathexis and those which have a negative cathexis; he no longer knows when or from what to withdraw. He has lost his freedom of choice, he cannot select appropriate means to his end goals, because he does not have the capacity to see the choices that are open to him.

2 NEUROTIC MECHANISMS

Birth of Neurosis

The individual's chance of physical survival is almost nil if he is left entirely to himself. Man needs others to survive physically. His psychological and emotional survival chances are even lower if he is left alone. On the psychological level, man needs *contact* with other human beings as much as, on the physiological level, he needs food and drink. Man's sense of relatedness to the group is as natural to him as his sense of relatedness to any one of his physiological survival impulses. Indeed, this sense of identification is probably his primary psychological survival impulse.

The gestalt approach, which considers the individual as a function of the organism/environment field, and which considers his behavior as reflecting his relatedness within that field, gives coherence to this conception of man as both an individual and as a social creature. The older psychologies described human life as a constant conflict between the individual and his environment. We see it, on the other hand, as an interaction between the two, within the framework of a constantly changing field. And since the field is constantly changing, out of its own nature and out of what we do to it, the forms and techniques of interaction must necessarily be fluid and changeable themselves.

What concerns us as psychologists and psychotherapists, in this ever-changing field, are the ever-changing constellations of the ever-changing individual. For he must change constantly if he is to survive. It is when the individual becomes incapable of altering his techniques of manipulation and interaction that neurosis arises. When the individual is frozen to an outmoded way of acting, he is less capable of meeting any of his survival needs, including his social needs. And the very large number of alienated, unidentified, and isolated individuals we find around us is ample evidence that this inability can easily arise. If we look at man in his environment, as both an individual and a social creature, as part of the organism/environment field, we cannot lay the blame for this alienation either at the door of the individual or of the environment. In our first chapter, in talking about the old mind-body problem, we pointed out that a causal relationship cannot exist among the elements that go to make up the whole. And since individual and environment are merely elements of a single whole, the field, neither of them can be held responsible for the ills of the other.

But both of them are ill. A society containing a large number of neurotic individuals must be a neurotic society; of the individuals living in a neurotic society, a large number must be neurotic. The man who can live in concernful contact with his society, neither being swallowed up by it nor withdrawing from it completely, is the well-integrated man. He is self-supportive because he understands the relationship between himself and his society, as the parts of the body instinctively seem to understand their relationship to the body-as-a-whole. He is the man who recognizes the contact boundary between himself and his society, who renders unto Caesar the things that are Caesar's and retains for himself those things that are his own. The goal of psychotherapy is to create just such men.

The ideal of a democratic community, on the other hand, is to create a society with the same characteristics, a community in which, as its needs are determined, each member participates for the benefit of all. Such a society is in concernful contact with its members. In such a society, the boundary between the individual and the group is clearly drawn and clearly felt. The individual is not subservient to the group nor is the group at the mercy of any individual. The principle of homeostasis, of self-regulation, also governs such a society. As the body responds to its dominant needs first, so would the society respond to its dominant needs first. If a fire threatened the whole community, everyone would help to extinguish the flames and salvage life and property. But, as the human-body-as-a-whole fights to preserve the integrity of any of its members when that one is under attack, so, in a well-regulated or self-regulated community, if the fire threatened only one home, the home owner's neighbors and, if necessary, the entire community would join with him in fighting it. The members of the community and its rulers would mutually identify with one another, and the members would identify with each other.

Man seems to be born with a sense of social and psychological balance as acute as his sense of physical balance. Every movement he makes on the social or psychological level is a movement in the direction of finding that balance, of establishing equilibrium between his personal needs and the demands of his society. His difficulties spring not from the desire to reject such equilibrium, but from misguided movements aimed towards finding and maintaining it.

When these movements bring him into severe conflict with society because, in his search for the contact boundary, (the point of balance) he has overshot the mark and impinged too heavily on society, we call him a criminal. The criminal is the man who has arrogated to himself functions traditionally defined as the prerogatives of the state. The man who arrogates these functions to himself is, in our society, a criminal.

When, on the other hand, man's search for balance leads him to draw back further and further, leads him to permit society to impinge too heavily on him, to overwhelm him with its demands and at the same time alienate him from social living, to push and passively mold him, we call him a neurotic. The neurotic cannot see his own needs clearly and therefore cannot fulfill them. He cannot distinguish properly between himself and the rest of the world, and he tends to see society as larger than life and himself as smaller. The criminal cannot see the needs of others—and therefore stamps on them—because he too cannot properly distinguish between himself and the rest of the world. As contrasted with the neurotic, he tends to see himself as larger than life and society as smaller.

What is it, then, in the organism/environment field, that permits such disturbances in balance to arise? Sociologists will examine this question in terms of the environment. Psychologists, psychiatrists, and psychotherapists examine it by examining what happens in the individual.

It seems to me that the imbalance arises when, simultaneously, the individual and the group experience differing needs, and when the individual is incapable of distinguishing which one is dominant. The group can mean the family, the state, the social circle, co-workers—any or all combinations of persons who have a particular functional relationship with one another at any given time. The individual, who is part of this group, experiences the need for contact with it as one of his primary psychological survival impulses, although of course he does not experience the need as acutely at all times. But when, at the same time, he experiences a personal need, the satisfaction of which requires withdrawal from the group, trouble can begin. In the situation of conflict of needs the individual has to be able to make a clear-cut decision. If he does this, he either stays in contact or he withdraws; he temporarily sacrifices the less dominant need to the more dominant, and that is that. Neither he nor the environment suffers any severe consequences. But when he cannot discriminate, when he cannot make a decision, or feel satisfied with the decision he has made, he can neither make a good contact nor a good withdrawal, and both he and the environment are affected.

There seems to be, in all human beings, an inborn tendency towards ritual, which can be defined as an expression of man's sense of social identification, his need for contact with a group. We find this tendency not only among primitives, but among highly civilized groups as well. The play of children is made up largely of ritual acting and repetition. Parades, festivals, religious services, all are expressions of this need. In a perverted way, the need for ritual seems to underlie the obsessional and compulsive neuroses—those that display themselves in such seemingly ridiculous needs as the compulsion to wash one's hands every twenty minutes. Obsessional rituals of this sort always have social as well as personal roots. But they maintain social form without social content, and at the same time, they are incapable of satisfying the individual's changing needs. They are the most sterile kind of expression—rendering nothing either to Caesar or to the self.

But normal people, too, seem to feel the need for ritual. If at an important occasion there were no ritual at all—no toast, no handshake, no speech, no processional, no ceremony of any kind—the whole thing would seem meaningless and flat. The ritual seems to give such experience order, form, and purpose. In gestalt terms, we could say that it makes the gestalt clearer, makes the figure stand out more sharply. All of us, for example, seem to feel the need for some ritual in dealing with death. Even the most sophisticated citizen of the world would find it shocking if we simply bundled our corpses up in bags and disposed of them.

At the same time that it satisfies a deep-seated need in the individual, the ritual has social value as well. For ritual reinforces the survival value of group living. It joins people together. Drill, for example, increases the coordination of its participants, and at the same time increases their capacity to act as a group in defense of their group needs. Magic—which is simply fantasized manipulation of the environment—serves to enhance the value of the group as a tool for the achievement of goals. It is used to evoke the support of beneficial powers (those that have a positive cathexis) and to annihilate dreaded powers (those that have a negative cathexis). Whatever the value for the group may be, ritual will—and it is meant to—interrupt at least some of the spontaneous and personal processes of the individuals in the group. Once engaged in ritual, all other activity is disesteemed as profane. The highest concentration, such as that befitting a dominant survival need, is demanded and achieved with solemnity and awe. Only a full participation of the entire personality will result in that religious feeling of intensified existence, of exaltation, of integration, without diminishing the full awareness of both the individual and the group, both the self and the other, and the full awareness of the individual that he is part of the group.

But such intensification of feeling is possible only if his full participation is uninterrupted. If there is any interruption at all—either from the environment, or if the individual interrupts in fantasy—the meaningfulness and integration of the entire activity is gone.

Now suppose that in the process of group activity, or ritual, the individual suddenly becomes aware of a personal survival need which appears more dominant than attention to the ritual. Suppose, for example, a chorus is in the middle of its performance, and one of its members suddenly finds that he has to urinate. His survival need profanely intrudes upon the solemn act. We then have three possibilities: the individual may withdraw (but quietly, so as not to call attention to himself), he may push his need completely into the background and force it, at least temporarily, out of existence, or he may vacillate in his attention from his own needs to the needs of the group. In this last case he tries to stay in contact with the ritual, to accord it the position of dominance, but he cannot, and a traumatic conflict between dread and impatience may occur. The sufferer might verbalize his experience thusly: "I want to urinate; I wish I could interrupt the session, but we want to go on. We don't like to be disturbed. And it isn't nice to disturb the others. So I wish I did not need to urinate, and I have to control myself. I wish my bladder would not bother me. It really is a nuisance."

In this apparently harmless statement lie hidden a whole series of confusions that can lead to neurosis. The speaker is apparently unable to distinguish properly between himself and his environment, and his statement contains all four of the mechanisms of meeting boundary disturbances that Gestalt therapy believes lie behind neurosis. This does not mean, of course, that he who utters it is a confirmed neurotic. It does mean that the attitudes which lie behind the statement, if they are unchecked, if they represent a continual pattern of thought and behavior, can develop into full-fledged neurotic attitudes. So let us leave our sufferer for a moment to discuss what these neurotic mechanisms are and how they develop. Then we can return to him and see how this simple situation can be the model for the development of neurotic patterns.

All neurotic disturbances arise from the individual's inability to find and maintain the proper balance between himself and the rest of the world, and all of them have in common the fact that in neurosis the social and environmental boundary is felt as extending too far over into the individual. The neurotic is the man on whom society impinges too heavily. His *neurosis* is a defensive maneuver to protect himself against the threat of being crowded out by an overwhelming world. It is his most effective technique for maintaining his balance and his sense of self-regulation in a situation where he feels that the odds are all against him.

Although we assume that the neuroses, the boundary disturbances, operate primarily through four mechanisms which can be distinguished, one from the other, it would be unrealistic to say that any particular kind of neurotic behavior was an example only of the operation of any single one of them. Nor would it be reasonable to say that any single confusion about the boundary—any single disturbance of the balance in the organism/environment field—produces neurosis or is evidence of a neurotic pattern. There are, to be sure, certain situations where this does occur, and they lead to what psychiatry calls the *traumatic neuroses*. The traumatic neuroses are essentially patterns of defense that originate in an attempt by the individual to protect himself from a thoroughly terrifying intrusion of society or clash with the environment. For example, the two-year-old child whose parents lock him in a dark closet overnight has been subjected to an almost insupportable strain. He has been reduced by their behavior to nothing—indeed, to less than nothing; to an object of manipulation with neither rights nor powers of his own. There is no "he" any more, there is only "they" and what "they" can do. In defending himself against this situation, the child is likely to develop rigid patterns of behavior. And these may persist long after the danger is past. They were called into action by a trauma, but they continue to operate even when the trauma itself has disappeared from existence.

But the boundary disturbances that lie behind most neuroses are usually less dramatic than this. They are nagging, chronic, daily interferences with the processes of growth and self-recognition through which we reach self-support and maturity. And whatever form these interferences and interruptions of growth may take, they result in the development of continuing confusion between the self and the other.

Introjection

All of us grow through exercising the capacity to discriminate, itself a function of the self-other boundary. We take from the environment, we give back to it. We accept or reject what the environment has to offer. We can only grow if, in the process of taking, we digest completely and we assimilate thoroughly. What we have really assimilated from our environment becomes ours, to do with as we please. We can retain it, or we can give it back in its new form, its distillation through us. But what we swallow whole, what we accept indiscriminately, what we ingest and do not ingest, is a foreign body, a parasite that is making its home in us. It is not part of us, even though it may look as if it is. It is still part of the environment.

Physically, this process of growth by assimilation—by destructuring and digesting—is easy to see. We grow and maintain ourselves not through the food we swallow whole, but through the food we chew (which begins the process of destructuring) and digest (which continues the process by further changing the food into chemical particles which the body can use). Physical food, then, properly digested and assimilated, becomes part of us—it is converted into bone, muscle, and blood. But food which is swallowed whole, which we shove down our gullets, not because we want it, but because we have to eat it, lies heavily on the stomach. It makes us uncomfortable, we want to throw it up and get it out of our systems. If we do not, if we suppress our discomfort, nausea, and desire to get rid of it, then we finally succeed either in painfully digesting it or else it poisons us.

The psychological process of assimilating is very much the same as its physiological counterpart. Concepts, facts, standards of behavior, morality, and ethical, esthetic or political values—all these come to us originally from the outside world. There is nothing in our minds that does not come from the environment, but there is nothing in the environment for which there is not an organismic need, physical or psychological. These must be digested and mastered if they are to become truly our own, truly a part of the personality. But if we simply accept them whole-hog and uncritically, on someone else's say-so, or because they are fashionable or safe or traditional or unfashionable or dangerous or revolutionary—they lie heavily on us. They are really undigestible. They are still foreign bodies even though they may have taken up residence in our minds. Such undigested attitudes, ways of acting, feeling and evaluating, psychology calls *introjects,* and the mechanism by which these alien accretions are added to the personality we call introjection.

I am not saying that this process of swallowing whole does not occasionally serve a useful purpose. The student who crams the night before an examination in order to get a passing grade in a very dull subject has a legitimate reason for his actions. But if he deludes himself into thinking that he has really learned anything from his cramming, he will be in for a bad shock when, six months later, he is again quizzed on the same subject. For by that time he will have lost the greatest part of what he "learned."

Nor am I saying that the individual should reject any psychological food that comes from the outside world. It is as impossible to feed off oneself psychologically as it is to feed off oneself physically. What I am saying is that the psychological food with which the outside world presents us—the food of facts and attitudes on which our personalities are built—has to be assimilated in exactly the same way as is our actual food. It has to be destructured, analyzed, taken apart, and then put together again in the form in which it will be of most value to us. If it is merely swallowed whole, it contributes not at all to the development of our personalities. On the contrary, it makes us something like a house so jampacked with other people's possessions that there is no room for the owner's property. It turns us into waste baskets of extraneous and irrelevant information. And what makes it most tragic is the fact that if this material were to be tempered, altered and transformed through us, it could be of enormous value to us.

The dangers of introjection, then, are twofold. First of all, the man who introjects never gets a chance to develop his own personality, because he is so busy holding down the foreign bodies lodged in his system. The more introjects he has saddled himself with, the less room there is for him to express or even discover what he himself is. And in the second place, introjection contributes to personality disintegration. If you swallow whole two incompatible concepts, you may find yourself torn to bits in the process of trying to reconcile them. And this is a fairly common experience today.

Our society, for example, teaches all of us from infancy two entirely different and apparently opposing sets of attitudes. One is the Golden Rule, "do unto others as you would have them do unto you." The other is the law of the survival of the fittest, which has been reduced to the slogan, "dog eat dog." If we were to introject both of these bits of dogma, we would wind up trying to be, at the same time, kind, gentle, undemanding, and wantonly aggressive. We would love our neighbors, but we wouldn't trust them any further than we could throw them. We would emulate the meek, and at the same time would be ruthless and sadistic. Those who do introject both of these concepts, or any other set of warring ideas, make a battleground of their own personalities. And the neurotic's internal conflict is usually fought to a stalemate, where neither side wins, where the personality is immobilized for any further growth and development.

Introjection, then, is the neurotic mechanism whereby

we incorporate into ourselves standards, attitudes, ways of acting and thinking, which are not truly ours. In introjection, we have moved the boundary between ourselves and the rest of the world so far inside ourselves that there is almost nothing of us left. To go back to the example in our last chapter of our suffering singer's statement, "It isn't nice to disturb the others," is an example of introjection. Who, after all, said that—he or they? Does he really believe that his own needs are so unimportant that the needs of the group must always be given preference? When the introjector says, "I think," he usually means, "they think."

Projection

The reverse of introjection is *projection.* As introjection is the tendency to make the self responsible for what actually is part of the environment, so projection is the tendency to make the environment responsible for what originates in the self. Clinically, we recognize that the disease of paranoia, which is characterized by the development of a highly organized system of delusions, is the extreme case of projection. The paranoiac has been found to be, in case after case, a highly aggressive personality who, unable to bear the responsibility for his own wishes, feelings, and desires, attaches them to objects or people in the environment. His conviction that he is being persecuted is in fact the statement that he would like to persecute others.

But projection exists in much less extreme forms than this, and we have to be careful to distinguish between projection, which is a pathological process, and assumption based on observation, which is normal and healthy. Planning and anticipating, skirmishing and maneuvering in a game of chess and many other activities all involve behavior based on observation and assumptions about the outside world. But these assumptions are recognized as assumptions. The chess player who thinks ahead several moves is making a whole group of assumptions about his opponent's mental processes based on his observations. Essentially, he is saying, "If I were he, this is what I would do." But he recognizes that he is making assumptions which will not necessarily govern his opponent's behavior, and he recognizes that these assumptions are his own.

On the other hand, the sexually inhibited woman who complains because everyone is making passes at her, or the cold, withdrawn, haughty man who accuses others of being unfriendly to him—these are examples of neurotic projection. In these cases the individuals have made assumptions based on their own fantasies and have failed to recognize that they are only assumptions. In addition, they have further refused to recognize the origin of their assumptions. Artistic creation, too, demands a kind of assumptive-projective behavior. The novelist often literally projects himself into his characters and becomes them while he is writing about them. But again, he does not suffer from the confusion of identity which characterizes the projecting neurotic. He knows where he leaves off and his characters begin, although in the heat of creative activity he may temporarily lose his sense of boundary and become someone else.

The neurotic does not use the mechanism of projection only in relation to his dealings with the world outside himself. He also uses it on himself. He has a tendency not only to disown his own impulses, but also to disown those parts of himself in which the impulses arise. He gives them, as it were, an objective existence outside himself so that he can make them responsible for his troubles without facing the fact that they are part of him. Instead of being an active participant in his own life the projector becomes a passive object, the victim of circumstances.

Our singer's plaintive statement about his bladder, "It really is a nuisance," is a neat little example of projection. The *it* has reared its ugly head; our fellow is on the verge of being victimized by his own bladder. "It just has to happen to me; I have to suffer," he is saying. We are witnessing the birth of a tiny bit of paranoia. For just as the answer to the introjector's question "who said that?" is "they," so the answer to the projector's statement is, "it's your bladder, it's you that wants to urinate." When the projector says "it" or "they" he usually means "I."

In projection, then, we shift the boundary between ourselves and the rest of the world a little too much in our own favor—in a manner that makes it possible for us to disavow and disown those aspects of our personalities which we find difficult or offensive or unattractive. And usually, by the way, it is our introjects that lead us to the feelings of self-contempt and self-alienation that produce projection. Because our hero has introjected the notion that good manners are more important than the satisfaction of pressing personal needs, because he has introjected the belief that one should learn to "grin and bear it," he must project or even expel those impulses in him which are at odds with what he now considers external activities. So no longer does he want to urinate; he is a good boy, he wants to stay with the group and continue singing. But that nasty, inconsiderate bladder, which just happens to have its residence in him, and which he now conceives of as being an introject—a foreign element introduced forcibly into him against his will—wants him to urinate. Like the introjector, he is incapable of distinguishing between those facets of his total personality which are really his and those which are imposed on him from the outside. He sees his introjects as himself and he sees those parts of himself which he would rather be rid of as undigested and indigestible introjects. By projecting, he hopes to rid himself of his fancied introjects, which are, in fact, not introjects at all, but aspects of himself.

The introjecting personality, who becomes a battleground for warring unassimilated ideas, is paralleled by the projecting personality, who makes the world the battleground on which his private conflicts must be fought out. The over-wary, over-cautious person, who tells you he wants friends and wants to be loved, but who tells you at the same time that "you can't trust anyone, they're all out for what they can get," is a projector par excellence.

Confluence

When the individual feels no boundary at all between himself and his environment, when he feels that he and it are one, he is in *confluence* with it. Parts and whole are indistinguishable from one another. Newborn infants live in confluence; they have no sense of any distinction between inside and outside, between the self and the other. In moments of ecstasy or extreme concentration, grown people, too, feel confluent with their environment. Ritual demands this sense of confluence, in which boundaries disappear and the individual feels most himself because he is so closely identified with the group. Part of the reason ritual produces a sense of exaltation and heightened experience is that normally we feel the self-other boundary quite sharply, and its temporary dissolution is consequently felt as a tremendously impactful thing. But when this sense of utter identification is chronic and the individual is unable to see the difference between himself and the rest of the world, he is psychologically sick. He cannot experience himself because he has lost all sense of himself.

The person in whom confluence is a pathological state cannot tell what he is and he cannot tell what other people are. He does not know where he leaves off and others begin. As he is unaware of the boundary between himself and others, he cannot make good contact with them. Nor can he withdraw from them. Indeed, he cannot even make contact with himself.

We are built from millions of cells. If we were a confluence, we would be a jelly-like mass and no organization would be possible. If, on the other hand, every cell were separated from one another by a porous membrane, then this membrane is the place of contact, of discrimination, as to what is "accepted" and what is "rejected."

If our component parts, however, which operate not only as parts of the total human being but also perform their own particular functions, are brought together and kept together in pathological confluence, neither will be able to perform its own job properly. Let us take as an example some chronic inhibition. Suppose that on several occasions you wanted to cry, but you prevented yourself from doing it by deliberately contracting the muscles of your diaphragm. Suppose further that this pattern of behavior, which originally arose as a conscious effort to suppress the need to cry, became habitual and unaware. The breathing and the need to cry would have become confused and confluent with one another. You would then have lost both activities—the capacity to breathe freely and the capacity to cry. Unable to sob, you would never release and work through your sorrow; probably after a while you would even forget what you were sad about. The need to sob and the contraction of the diaphragm as a defense against the expression of this need together form a single stabilized battle line of activity and counteractivity, and this perpetual warfare goes on constantly, and in isolation from the rest of the personality. The man who is in pathological confluence ties up his needs, his emotions, and his activities in one bundle of utter confusion until he is no longer aware of what he wants to do and how he is preventing himself from doing it. Such pathological confluence lies behind many of the diseases now recognized as psychosomatic. The breathing-sobbing confusion we mentioned above may lead to asthma, if it persists long enough.

Pathological confluence has serious social consequences, too. In confluence, one demands likeness and refuses to tolerate any differences. We often find this in parents who consider their children to be merely extensions of themselves. Such parents lack the appreciation that their children are bound to be unlike them in at least some respects. And if the children are not confluent, and do not identify with their parents' demands, they will meet with rejection and alienation: "You are not my son." "I don't love such a naughty child."

If the members of the United Nations were to appreciate or even esteem the differences between the nations that go to make up the organization, they would have good contact, and there would be a good chance of working out the problems that now beset the world. But as long as differences are not tolerated, and as long as each nation demands that all the others should share its outlook, point for point, conflict and confusion will continue. As long as differences are not appreciated, they are likely to be persecuted. The demand for total agreement, for confluence, is like the statement, "If you won't be my friend, I'll crack your skull open!"

Our singer's statement, "We want to go on," when in fact it is they who want to go on and not he—he wants to leave and urinate—is a statement of confluence; a statement that he no longer knows how to distinguish between himself and the rest of the group. When the man who is in pathological confluence says "we" you can't tell who he is talking about; himself or the rest of the world. He has completely lost all sense of boundary.

Retroflection

The fourth neurotic mechanism can be called *retroflection,* which literally means "turning back sharply against." The retroflector knows how to draw a boundary line between himself and the environment, and he draws a neat and clean one right down the middle—but he draws it down the middle of himself. *The introjector does as others would like him to do, the projector does unto others what he accuses them of doing to him, the man in pathological confluence doesn't know who is doing what to whom, and the retroflector does to himself what he would like to do to others.* When a person retroflects behavior, he treats himself as he originally wanted to treat other persons or objects. He stops directing his energies outward in attempts to manipulate and bring about changes in the environment that will satisfy his needs; instead, he redirects his activity inwards and substitutes himself in place of the environment as the target for behavior. To the extent that he does this, he splits his personality into doer and done to. He literally becomes his own worst enemy.

Obviously, no human being can go through life giving free reign to every one of his impulses. At least some of them have to be held in check. But deliberately resisting destructive impulses with the recognition that they are destructive is quite different from turning them against oneself. The harassed mother at the tail end of a long and hectic day in which the washing machine went berserk and tore the clothes, her five-year-old son went berserk and scribbled with red crayon all over the living room wall, the man who was supposed to fix the vacuum cleaner didn't show up and her husband came home an hour late for dinner is likely to feel absolutely murderous. It would not be advisable for her to kill the child or her husband, but it would be equally foolish for her to cut her own throat.

How does the mechanism of retroflection display itself? As introjection displays itself in the use of the pronoun "I" when the real meaning is "they"; as projection displays itself in the use of the pronouns "it" or "they," when the real meaning is "I"; as confluence displays itself in the use of the pronoun "we" when the real meaning is in question; so retroflection displays itself in the use of the reflective, "myself."

The retroflector says, "I am ashamed of myself," or "I have to force myself to do this job." He makes an almost endless series of statements of this sort, all of them based on the surprising conception that he and himself are two different people. What does our singer say? "I must control myself."

The confusion between the self and the other that lies behind neurosis shows itself also in utter confusion about the self. To the neurotic, the self is a beast or an angel—but the self is never myself.

Freud in describing the development of personality contributed to this confusion. He talked about the ego, (the "I") the id, (the organic drives) and the superego, (the conscience) and described the individual's psychic life as a constant conflict between them—clenched in an endless and unbreakable embrace with himself—man struggles until death. The retroflector seems to be acting in accordance with the Freudian picture of man. But stop to consider for a moment what the super-ego actually is. If it is not part of the self, the "I," the ego, it must of necessity be a bundle of introjects, of unassimilated attitudes and approaches imposed on the individual by the environment. Freud talks of introjection as part of the moral process of growth; he says for example that the child introjects the "good" parent images and establishes them as his ego-ideals. The ego, then, becomes a bundle of introjects too. But study after study of neurotic personalities shows us that problems arise not in relation to a childhood identification with "good" parents, but in relation to identification with the "bad" parents. The child does not, in fact, introject the attitudes and ethics of the "good" parents. He assimilates them. He may not be aware in complicated terms and psychiatric jargon of what he is doing, but he is translating the attitudes that lie behind his parents' satisfying behavior into terms which he can understand; reducing them, as it were, to the least common denominator, and then assimilating them in their new form, a form which he can use. He cannot comparably reduce his parents' "bad" attitudes; he has no means for coping with them, and certainly no built-in desire to cope with them. So he must take them over as undigested introjects. And that is where the trouble begins. For now we have a personality made up, not of ego and super-ego, but of I and not I, of self and self-image, a personality so confused that it has become incapable of distinguishing one from the other.

Indeed, this confusion of identification is in fact neurosis. And whether it displays itself primarily through the use of the mechanism of introjection or of projection or of retroflection or of confluence, its hallmark is disintegration of the personality and lack of coordination in thought and action.

Therapy consists in rectifying false identifications. If neurosis is the product of "bad" identifications, health is the product of "good" identifications. That leaves open, of course, the question of which are the good identifications and which are the bad. The simplest and, I think, the most satisfactory answer—and one based on observable reality—is that "good" identifications are those which promote the satisfactions and goal-fulfillments of the individual and his environment. And "bad" identifications are those which result in stunting or thwarting the individual, or destructive behavior toward his environment. For the neurotic not only makes himself miserable, he punishes all those who care for him by his self-destructive behavior.

In therapy, then, we have to re-establish the neurotic's capacity to discriminate. We have to help him to rediscover what is himself and what is not himself; what fulfills him and what thwarts him. We have to guide him towards integration. We have to assist him in finding the proper balance and boundary between himself and the rest of the world. It is simple to say, "just be yourself," but for the neurotic, a thousand obstacles bar the way. Understanding now, as we do, the mechanisms through which the neurotic is preventing himself from being himself, we can settle down to try to remove the road blocks, one by one. For this is what should happen in therapy, and therapy is what we shall now discuss.

3 HERE COMES THE NEUROTIC

And now here comes our neurotic—tied to the past and to outmoded ways of acting, fuzzy about the present because he sees it only through a glass darkly, tortured about the future because the present is out of his hands. Into the consultation room he walks, shame-faced or brazen, shy or bold, dragging his feet or trying to step jauntily. To him the therapist may be a disembodied pair of ears, or perhaps a fairy godfather who has but to wave his magic wand to transform the beast into a beautiful young man, handsome of feature, long of limb, and loaded with cash and charm. Or maybe he suspects that the therapist is nothing but a fraud and a charlatan, but is willing, out of the despair of his problem and the goodness of his heart, to give him one quick chance.

Whatever fantasies flit through his head as he approaches, whatever appearance he presents, the patient comes for treatment because he feels that he is in an *existential crisis*—that is, he feels that the psychological needs with which he has identified himself, and which are as vital to him as breath itself, are not being met by his present mode of life. The psychological needs that assume this life-or-death importance are as many and as varied as the patients themselves. To one, keeping up with the Jonses and surpassing them, if possible, is a dominant need. Such a person identifies his total existence with his social existence, and if his social position is threatened he is in an existential crisis. To another, having the single-minded devotion of wife, husband, or lover is a dominant need. If such a person cannot achieve this goal, or having achieved it, loses it, he is in an existential crisis. To one neurotic, "self-control" is an existential need; to another, "self-expression." Whatever the existential needs are, the fact that he comes for therapy is the patient's admission that they are not being met. He consults the therapist because he hopes to find in him the environmental support that will supplement his own inadequate means of support.

He thinks that with the therapist's help he will be able to satisfy these needs which neither he nor his environment can now satisfactorily meet. He feels as if he is in a bottomless pit. This may be because he has set himself an impossible task. Then, in the course of successful therapy, his goals will alter; his existential needs will change. It may be because his experience and training have not developed in him enough self-support to make it possible for him to attain fairly simple goals on his own. Then successful therapy will give him greater self-support.

It is not the therapist's task to make value judgments about his patients' existential needs. The therapist may not be particularly interested in business, but if his patient feels success in business to be an existential need, the therapist must help him to achieve the self-support that will make this goal possible. It is not the therapist's task to reduce all his patients to uniformity, to present them all with the same set of existential needs, tailor-made to fit either the least or most competent of them. His task is to facilitate for each of them the development that will enable them to find goals that are meaningful to them and to work towards these goals in a mature way. For, as of the moment when he begins therapy, the patient cannot do these things for himself.

His homeostasis is not working properly; he flails, he rushes about, and like Alice he has to run like the wind to stay where he is. But it is working well enough so that the imbalance produces a need to right it, and this need is felt as a *positive cathexis* of the therapist.

Well, what does the patient need from us? A wailing wall, a shoulder to cry on? An ally to condemn his wife or his boss, a patient listener? Somebody to punish him for his sins or, if he has punished himself enough already, to forgive and to redeem him? Does he need reassurance, a shot of confidence? Is he dreaming of acquiring magical power of submitting to a painless wonder cure? Does he want reinforcement of his self-control, an increase of his sexual potency, a short-cut to happiness? Does he want appreciation or love, a prop for his lacking self-esteem, rescue from the boredom of life, salvation from intolerable loneliness, improvement of his memory? Does he want meanings and interpretations, hoping that they will bring about understanding of himself? Or does he want confirmation of his feeling that he is such a sick person that he cannot fight life all alone?

Whatever it is, he cannot secure it for himself and, apparently, he cannot secure it from his environment. Otherwise he would not have come to the therapist. But he certainly has tried to get the support he needs, and certainly he has been partially successful. If he had failed completely, he would be mad or dead. To the degree that he has not succeeded, however, he comes to us frustrated and without having achieved full satisfaction.

However, he does not come empty-handed. He brings with him his means of *manipulation*, his ways of mobilizing and using his environment to do his work for him. And let us not delude ourselves into thinking that these manipulatory techniques are not clever. The neurotic is not a fool. He has to be pretty shrewd in order to survive since in fact he is lacking, to a marked degree, one of the essential qualities that promotes survival—self-support. He literally has a handicap, and it takes considerable ingenuity to get along with it. Unfortunately, however, all his maneuvers are directed towards minimizing its effects instead of overcoming it. The maneuvers may have been deliberate at one time and by now be so habitual that the neurotic is no longer aware of them, but that does not mean that they are not maneuvers and that they are not clever. We recognize the shrewdness of the platinum blonde babe who coaxes diamonds and minks out of a sugar daddy. The whiny, dependent woman who coaxes attention and support out of her husband, her children, and even her acquaintances is no less shrewd. We acknowledge the cleverness of the politician who rides roughshod over his opposition. The desensitized neurotic who is blind and deaf to what he does not want to know is equally clever. The neurotic's problem is not that he cannot manipulate, but that his manipulations are directed towards preserving and cherishing his handicap, rather than getting rid of it. If he learns how to devote as much intelligence and energy to becoming self-supportive as he does to making his environment support him, he cannot but succeed.

For his capacities to manipulate are his achievements, they are his pluses, as his inability to meet his existential crisis is his minus. And it is from his pluses that we can start to build. When the patient becomes aware that he is manipulating his environment in a fashion that, no matter how intricate, is self-defeating, and when he becomes aware of his manipulatory techniques themselves, he will be able to make changes.

His *means of manipulation* are manifold. He can talk, often drowning us with words. He can sulk and go on strike. He can promise and make resolutions; he can break promises and resolutions. He can be subservient, he can sabotage. He can hear the slightest nuances, or he can play deaf. He can remember or he can forget, as the situation requires. He can pull the wool over our eyes and lead us up the primrose path. He can lie and he can be compulsively honest. He can move us to tears with his misery, or he can bear his fate with a stiff upper lip. He can hypnotize us with his monotonous voice or he can irritate us with his shrillness. He can flatter our vanity and hurt our pride. He can, as long as he himself is left out, bring us his "problems" neatly wrapped in a parcel adorned with the flowers of his psychological jargon, expecting us to unwrap it for him and to explain the contents of the package to his satisfaction. If the therapist is an intellectualizer, the patient will argue until doomsday; if he is looking for a childhood trauma, the patient will help with true or manufactured instances. If the therapist is keen on transferences, the patient will make everybody his pappa and mamma, with a few siblings to be rivaled for good measure.

Most of all he manipulates with dissociations and with questions. If we point out that he does not produce any relevant associations, he accuses us of a breach of faith, because what he said was what came into his mind. But was he really so unaware of interrupting and avoiding the relevant? As to his questions, their functions are innumerable. Masked as an appeal to our omniscience, they are intended to pump us for information which is forgotten a minute later; they test us, they are intended to embarrass and entrap us—they are the patient's main tools for not coming to grips with his problems. As such, they are very valuable indications of the areas of his confusion and, properly handled, provide us with an excellent counter-tool.

But what about the negative cathexis, the patient's fear that therapy, instead of helping him, will plunge him even deeper into a no-man's land, will completely knock the props out from under him? It is, roughly—but very roughly—related to the phenomenon of resistance. Such a resemblance must not deceive us, however. We must not fall into the trap of believing that resistances are bad and that the patient would be better off without them. On the contrary, resistances are as valuable to us as the resistance movements were to the Allies during the Second World War. Otto Rank very properly called resistance negative will. If the therapist disapproves of resistances, he might as well give up. It does not matter whether he expresses his disapproval openly or not; the patient's intuition is seldom so dulled that he does not feel it. The neurotic, like everyone else, is geared to live by manipulation of his environment. Because he usually sees the environment as hostile he is often very sensitive and ready to outguess, outfeel, and outwit his opponent. He easily penetrates the mask of those orthodox analysts who, in dread of a counter-transference, have de-emotionalized themselves. Shrinking from any contact, dead as dinosaurs, they present the patient with a poker-face. Anyway, the patient does not think of his resistance as resistance; he usually experiences it as assistance. He wants to help.

For what he dreads is rejection, disapproval, and ultimate dismissal by the therapist (the brazen ones, of course, do not permit this to show). So the patient manipulates the therapist by putting on the appearance of the good child. He tries to bribe the therapist with submission and pseudo-acceptance of his wisdom and his requests. At the same time, he may have a very unstable self esteem, he may be very sensitive to real or imagined criticism. So he gets tense every time the therapist speaks to him.

The patient has taken great pains to build up a self-concept. This self-concept is well known in psychiatry under such names as reaction-formation, self-system, ego-ideal, persona, and what not. It is often a completely erroneous concept of himself, each feature representing the exact opposite of its actuality. This self-concept can give the patient no support whatsoever; on the contrary, he is busy nagging, disapproving of himself, squashing anything of genuine self-expression. He not only exhausts himself in this Sisyphus struggle, but he also needs the permanent environmental support of approval and acceptance. He has projected his own power of discrimination, that is, his capacity to accept or reject, to such a degree that any pat on the back, no matter from whom it comes, is welcome. He has also foregone his ability to accept genuinely, so no praise is assimilated, and he remains greedy and dissatisfied with whatever affection he gets.

This is a striking example of how lacking the support of self-esteem will result in a constant need for external support—the need to be esteemed by others. And because this environmental support is sought for the self-concept, it can never contribute to the growth of the self. *Man transcends himself only via his true nature, not through ambition and artificial goals.* They lead, at best, to pride and vainglory.

The true nature of man, like the true nature of any other animal, is integrity. Only in an integrated spontaneity and deliberateness does he make a sound existential choice. For both spontaneity and deliberation are in the nature of man. Awareness of and responsibility for the total field, for the self as well as the other, these give meaning and pattern to the individual's life.

So much has been written about the superstructure of the self-concept under such names as over-compensation, the inferiority and superiority complexes, and so on, that it has become one of the most thoroughly examined phenomena of psychiatry. Even the layman talks about his "second nature." Yet with all the discussion of the self-concept and its superstructure, therapy only rarely achieves a true penetration to the self. In my opinion this is because in most forms of therapy not enough attention is paid to the layer of confusion which separates the self from the self-concept. Since confusion is extremely unpleasant, it works as a powerful deterrent, and the patient mobilizes every means at his disposal to avoid viewing clearly his areas of confusion. In this respect he behaves quite differently from Socrates, who freely admitted his intellectual and existential confusions, and who dedicated his life to, and developed, a technique of deconfusing.

Confusion is a matter of inadequate orientation, and unacknowledged confusion is one of the characteristics of neurosis. Any action based on confusion will show embarrassment, faltering, and disturbances of all kinds. When we are confused and do not know it, we have no freedom of choice, we deal with our experiences as if certain specific techniques of manipulation were necessities and absolutes. Psychiatry has devoted a good deal of attention to the ambivalence confusion, where the patient feels that he should either love or hate, that he is either good or bad. We merely have to replace the either/or by "this as well as that," and we are in the clear, making the positive or negative cathexis dependent on the context in which it occurs. We can love one moment and feel good, and we can hate the next and feel bad, depending on the satisfactions or frustrations involved in the situation. Ambivalence presupposes that states of permanent satisfaction or frustration exist. It is again a *static concept*—as if our emotions could be petrified in time or as if we ourselves could be petrified in time.

In therapy, if the environmental support the patient expects from us is not forthcoming, if we don't give him the answers he thinks he has to have, if we don't appreciate his good intentions, admire his psychological knowledge, congratulate him on his progress, we shall get the negative cathexis of frustration. But Gestalt therapy also constantly gives him much of what he wants—attention, exclusive attention—and we don't blame him for his resistances. In this way therapy starts out with a certain balance of frustration and satisfaction.

The field is now set for the therapeutic operation. What shall we do with our patient? Is he to lie down on the couch, close his eyes, and associate freely? Do we ask him to dwell on his recollections of the Oedipal phase, his interpersonal relations, his motor armor? Are we concerned with his past or his present, his capacity to flit from subject to subject in a flight of ideas or to concentrate steadily on any one for even a brief time? Are we dealing with his mind or his body? Are we to worry about why he censors and interrupts himself and his expressions, or how? Shall we deal with the subterranean depths of his personality, or with his surface? Are we to depend on his words or his actions? Do we treat his physical symptoms in psychological terms or his psychological symptoms in physical terms? Shall we observe him or interpret him? Is he to learn through his own experience or are we going to lecture him after he provides us with the subject matter for our dissertation?

The techniques of the conventional therapies are based on the theory that what the patient lacks is an understanding of the whys of his behavior, and that these whys can be uncovered if we dig deeply enough into the past, into his dreams, and into his unconscious. Depending on the therapist's affiliation, these whys may be any one of a number of factors, separately or in combination. Freud, for example, made certain observations leading to the theory of the Oedipus Complex as the dominant source of problems; Reich spoke in terms of the motor armor and the need for orgastic potency; Sullivan in terms of the self-system and interpersonal relationships; Salter in terms of the need for self-expression; Adler in terms of the inferiority complex; and so on.

Each of these contributions is valid, but all of them miss the basic point because they are still limited by an approach which does not see the organism/environment field as a whole. All of them are abstractions from the total process.

The Sullivanians come closest to taking into account the play of the field itself, but even here the emphasis is distorted by the basic dualism of the concept. Our approach, which sees the human being as simultaneously and by nature both an individual and a member of the group, gives us a broader base of operations. Let me repeat once again our explanation: A neurosis is a state of imbalance in the individual that arises when simultaneously he and the group of which he is a member experience differing needs and the individual cannot tell which is dominant. If this kind of experience is repeated often enough, or if a single experience of this sort is impressive enough, the individual's sense of balance in the field will become sufficiently disturbed so that he loses the ability in any situation to judge the balance position properly. He will then respond in a neurotic way to situations which have no intrinsic connection with the experience or experiences in which the imbalance initially arose. The neurotic's general way of meeting situations is to interrupt himself; the criminal's pattern is to interrupt the environment.

Our broader definition does not lead us to look for a single cause for neurotic behavior. We therefore reject as definitive answers any of the specific constellations which the other schools advance.

In traditional therapy, the assumption is that by recalling and reinterpreting the events of the past, therapist and patient together can piece out the effects of the patient's experiences on him, and that once they have done this, the patient will no longer be disturbed by his problems. He will either learn how to live with them or he will resolve them.

These assumptions seem to us invalid for several reasons. In the first place, therapy based on any assumption of a single set of simple "causes" concentrates on those aspects of the personality which are related to these "causes" and is blind to all of the other factors. Its own orientation is as limited as the patient's. It may improve his ability to get around within the limitations imposed jointly by his neurosis and the theory, but it does not open up broader areas of awareness. In other words, it is as if both patient and therapist were wearing blinders with magnifying glasses attached to them. Their vision directly ahead may be acute, but they see nothing of what is happening on either side. And the either/or emphasis on "mental" and "physical" —with most schools dealing with mental factors and the Reichians dealing with physical factors—limits the patient's increased maneuverability within the limited field and limits the therapist's ability to handle it.

The unitary Gestalt approach, on the other hand, makes it possible to increase the breadth of orientation and to improve the means of the therapeutic maneuvering. We believe that any situation or situations—acute or chronic—which the individual has learned to handle by an unsatisfactory process of self-interruption can lie behind neurosis. We cannot settle for any single "cause." We believe further that the "mental-physical" or "mind-body" split is a totally artificial one, and that to concentrate on either term in this false dichotomy is to preserve neurosis, not to cure it.

Since in our terms, fantasy is diminished reality and thinking is diminished acting, we can use fantasizing in a therapeutic way as it relates to acting, and we can use acting out in a therapeutic way as it relates to fantasizing. Our patients often use fantasies in a harmful way as a vicarious means of satisfying real needs; we can teach them to use it therapeutically to discover and satisfy real needs.

A second reason we feel therapy oriented to the past is invalid is because the *whys* of the patient's neurosis really explain very little. Why does a situation produce neurosis in Mr. A while the same situation leaves Mr. B untouched? Why did the situation arise in the first place? And why did the circumstances come into existence that created it? "Why" opens up an endless series of questions which can only be answered by a first cause that is self-caused. If a man is neurotic "because" his mother died in childbirth and he was raised by a stern maiden aunt who gave him no chance to do anything he wanted, and this forced him to repress certain desires, how will an explanation which makes the aunt the villain in the piece solve his problems? On the contrary, such an explanation only gives the patient license to project all his difficulties onto the aunt. It gives him a scapegoat, not an answer. And this kind of scapegoatism is very often the result of many orthodox therapies.

But there is a valuable clue to therapy in the recital of the facts of this case, and this is related to the next point. If the aunt did not let him do the things he wanted, his childhood was a constant series of interruptions, both from the outside, the aunt, and from the inside, himself. If our patient learns the *how* of his own interruptions—past and present—if he actually experiences himself interrupting himself, and feels the ways in which he is doing it, he can work through his interruptions into his real self and the activities he wants to carry out.

If therapy is successful, it will leave the patient self-supportive, no longer at the mercy of interrupting forces he cannot control. Additionally, problems are caused not only by what we have repressed but by those things about ourselves which our self-interruptions have prevented us from learning. Many of the neurotic's difficulties are related to his unawareness, his blind spots, to the things and relationships he simply does not sense. And therefore, rather than talking of the unconscious, we prefer to talk about the *at-this-moment-unaware*. This term is much broader and wider than the term "unconscious". This unawareness contains not only repressed material, but material which never came into awareness, and material which has faded or has been assimilated or has been built into larger gestalts. The unaware includes skills, patterns of behavior, motoric and verbal habits, blind spots, etc.

As the conscious is purely mental in nature, so is the unconscious. But the awareness and unawareness are not purely mental. In terms of our definition, both awareness and unawareness seem to be a property of protoplasm, of which all living creatures are composed. In so complex a creature as man, the areas of unawareness are quite wide. We are unaware of our vegetative processes, of the forces that impel us to breathe, to eat, and to excrete. We are unaware of many of the processes of growth. But as our areas of unawareness are wide, so are our areas of awareness; they include not only our overt sensory and motor activities, but also many of those faded activities we describe as mental.

A school of psychotherapy which has a unitary approach to the unitary organism, man, cannot concern itself only with mental material, repressed or expressed. It must concern itself with the total pattern of behavior, and must direct itself towards making the patient aware of as much of that total pattern as is necessary for health. Thus, as opposed to the orthodox schools, which put their emphasis on what the patient does not know about himself, we put ours on what he does know—on his areas of awareness, rather than his areas of unawareness. Our hope is to increase his awareness of himself progressively on all levels.

Perhaps the meaning of this difference in approach can be seen best in a discussion of what has become in recent years one of the most fashionable terms in psychiatry and cocktail party conversation: psychosomatic. What is a psychosomatic manifestation? If we maintain the old mind-body split to which the highly limited concept of the unconscious is so closely related, we can describe it either as a somatic disturbance related to a psychic event or as a psychic disturbance caused by a somatic event. But with our unitary point of view we do not have to fall into this trap of causality. We describe a psychosomatic event as one in which the gross physical disturbances are more impressive than the ones that occur on a mental or emotional level. The laws of support, contact, and interruption apply to each level; it is impossible to draw a line between psychosomatic manifestations and psychosomatic illness. Forgetting, for example, is a psychosomatic manifestation, but I doubt whether the most union-conscious M.D. would claim this symptom as belonging in his orbit. On the other hand, there are many instances of severe psychosomatic manifestations, such as ulcers, asthma and colitis, which require the support of drugs and medical care.

Let me discuss for a moment one of the classic psychosomatic manifestations, the headache. Headaches are used as excuses for withdrawal in thousands of cases in daily life. But except for the outright chronic liar, the headache is not only an excuse. In each case there is likely to be a genuine physical experience, a body language which says, "this situation gives me a headache," or "you make me sick." The headache is part of the whole interruption of contact mechanism. Each bit of excitement the organism creates at any given moment should enable it to cope with the actual situation through the transformation of the excitement into emotion and relevant action. But if the excitement is directed against the self, a supportive function is changed into an inhibition and so is bound to create a psychosomatic manifestation, or even a symptom. We try to deal with the totality of the headache experience, we do not shrug it off as a trivial symptom nor can we dispose of it permanently with drugs. We believe that such a psychosomatic manifestation deserves attention in psychotherapy. Nor, as you will see later, do we have to resort to interpreting the patient's "unconscious motivation" to deal with it.

To the orthodox therapist transference is the explanation of the therapeutic process. The neurotic, according to Freud, transfers onto the therapist a series of emotional responses and attitudes the patient once displayed in his dealings with a person or persons from the past. Thus, in transference the patient is acting out a form of delusion; what he believes to be personal contact with the therapist is actually an intra-organismic event of his own making. It is not *contact*, but something that prevents contact. For contact involves appreciation of what the other actually is, not what one construes him to be.

Yet this explanation, despite its great value, does not fully explicate the feelings the patient often develops towards the therapist in the course of treatment. Are we to assume that they have no actuality, that everything the patient feels is unreal, to be explained away by his history? Is there no being or becoming?

If we follow up the concept of cathexis, which originated with Freud, and apply it to the transference situation, we come to a conclusion directly opposite his. What is active in therapy is not what *has been;* on the contrary, it is precisely what has *not been*—a deficit or something missed. What has been is a finished situation. It progresses through satisfaction and integration into the making of the self. The unfinished situation, which is the failure of development from environmental to self-support, is the heritage of the past which remains in the present.

In other words, we maintain that transference, with its relations of actual feeling plus the patient's fantasied hopes, plus the expected support (which the patient takes for granted) stems from his "lack of being," and not from what was and has been forgotten. Our history is the background of our existence, it is not an accumulation of facts but the record of how we become what we are. Only the disturbances in the background that interfere with supporting our present lives push forward and have to become foreground so that they can be attended to. Then they can change from being deficiencies (incomplete gestalts) into support functions.

In the beginning of therapy, few patients will ask much support of the therapist. They are ready to burst, if we only give them the opportunity. But their lack of being appears increasingly as therapy progresses and the patient steps up his demands and manipulations. The therapist receives more and more cathexis—positive or negative—as he more and more symbolizes what the patient lacks.

What does this mean in the techniques of therapy? Let us take the case of a patient whose transference the orthodox therapist would describe as very strong, and whom I would describe as feeling that the therapist represents his entire lack of being. Such a patient frequently shows the following pattern: he wants to become a therapist; he is eager to use psychiatric jargon; he takes over the therapist's manner and style. If the therapist works in terms of the classical definition of transference, he will look for the historical precedents for this action, for the individual in the patient's past towards whom he displayed this same kind of introjecting behavior. He will look for *substance,* and having found it will hope that the patient eventually will learn to differentiate himself from the introjected other, who may be his mother or his father. But we, on the other hand, will look at the *process* rather than the substance. For the process is active today, as it was in the past. We will concentrate on the fact that, as an introjector, he looks for shortcuts, that he is lazy in assimilating the world, and that he interferes with his growth and self-realization. For as long as the patient is an accumulation of introjects, he is not he and he cannot support himself. For as long as he persists in the pattern of introjecting, support will be lacking. If introjection is his primary technique for meeting the world, even if we are successful in exorcising one or two introjects—pappa and mamma, for instance, he will still go on accumulating others. So we must concentrate on getting him to see how he swallows whole, how he consistently interrupts the process of destructuring and assimilating.

With a unitary approach we can handle this problem on both the levels of fantasy and actuality. As I pointed out earlier, if the organism swallows something it cannot assimilate, it will normally vomit up the undigestible stuff. The emotional side of this vomiting up is called disgust. By erecting some type of an inner barrier against the disgust, he fails to feel it. How does he build such a barrier? The patient either desensitizes himself or he avoids the experience by an elaborate system of over-estheticism. The introjector has to learn what the experience of disgust is, for it is by interrupting—feeling it that he continues to "swallow" others. If we can help him to become aware of his disgust and to see that it is due to swallowing whole the advice or values of another, the path is cleared for him to get relief from disgust, and to create himself, his own decisions, roles, and other potentials.

This does not mean that it is not equally important for him to learn that the therapist is not mamma or pappa or, in general, what the difference is between him and other people. But this he learns as he learns that he introjects and *how* he introjects. As he learns this, he also learns that his introjects are not his authentic self.

Full support for the self—overcoming the need for environmental support—can come only through making creative use of the energies that are invested in the blocks that prevent self-support. Instead of permitting our patients to see themselves passively transferring from the past, we have to introduce the mentality of responsibility, which says: "I am preventing myself . . ." "how do I prevent myself," and "from what do I prevent myself?"

If the therapist gives the patient environmental support—in other words, supports his transference need—he is only playing into the hands of the patient's neurosis. But if, on the other hand, he makes it possible for the patient to assimilate the blocking and the blocked material through identifying himself with it and differentiating himself from it, he facilitates the patient's development.

We must use the same approach to the dream, that fascinating bit of human creation that provides both patient and therapist, in orthodox analysis, with hundreds of hours of mouth-watering talk. Freud described the dream as a wish fulfillment and assumed that by shuttling between the content of the dream and its associations, its meaning would become clear. For although we know that the dream is our own creation, it is usually not meaningful to us; it seems to come from a strange world of its own.

But an explanation of the dream merely as wish fulfillment and a reduction of the dream to a series of crude verbal symbols seems to go against the very essence of the aliveness of the dream. Take the nightmare, for example. True, if you bracket it off into a series of static pieces, you can isolate the wish hidden among the horrors. Or you can come closer to Freud's contention that the entire dream is a wish fulfillment by calling it instead the interruption of a wish. But at face value it is absurd to call the whole nightmare a wish fulfillment.

The dream seems to be instead (and this applies not only to the nightmare, but to all dreams), rather an attempt to find a solution to an apparent paradox. The dream is an artistic creation in which two seemingly incompatible strivings are set against one another. In the nightmare, the paradox is not integrated; in the neurotic's daily life his paradoxes, too, remain unintegrated. Harry Stack Sullivan has pointed out that if we could solve our problems during the day we would not need to dream at night.

To make sense of the dream, we do well not to interpret it. Instead of speculating about it, we ask our patients to live it more extensively and intensively, to discover the paradox. In an orthodox analysis, through association, the patient extends his dream. From a short descriptive passage of one of his own dreams, Freud derived page on page of associations and interpretations. But to intensify the dream—to attempt to relive it—the patient must be open to much more than purely verbal interpretations and what comes into his mind; he has to admit sensations, emotions, and gestures as well. He can only integrate the dream and come to a solution of the paradox by re-identification, particularly with the interfering aspects of the dream.

Most psychiatric schools agree that the dream is a projection, that all the characters and objects that appear in it are actually the dreamer himself, and that the dream action is often an attempt to solve a paradox by disowning responsibility for one's own hopes and desires. The dream that one's enemy has been murdered by someone else is a perfect example of this.

Let me give you two specific instances of how we work with dreams. In both cases the reader will note that we ask the patient to identify with all the parts in his dream, and to try to become aware of the paradox it represents and to solve it.

In the first case, a young woman patient presented this dream: "I am going upstairs with a bundle under my arm." Her fantasies, as she identified with the different objects in the dream were: "If I am the staircase, somebody is using me to get on top. That's my husband, of course, who is ambitious and is now studying. He depends on me to help financially. If I am the bundle, then he has to carry me. This is also true. He has to take me along to the intellectual heights he is going to reach." Here we see what appears to the patient to be the paradox of her life situation: she is carrying a load and at the same time she is a load.

In the following case we tried to work out, in the therapeutic session, some solution to the paradox involved in the dream: A man patient presented a dream in which he saw a man pushing down some garbage that had clogged up a toilet bowl. He pushed and pushed until finally the entire toilet fell through the floor. There is room for much interpretation here; the action fitted in well with the patient's entire attitude towards the unpleasant. But instead of interpreting the dream for him, I asked the patient what, if he were the man in his dream, he could have done instead. He replied that he could take a hook and extract whatever was clogging the bowl. Then, by fantasizing this, he exposed all the disgusting material to his view. Immediately thereafter he felt a constriction in his throat which corresponded to the bottleneck of the toilet bowl. By constricting his throat he prevented himself from vomiting, from bringing up the disgusting material. Thus the dream content, his behavior, and the psychosomatic symptom became integrated. The underlying paradox—the paradox of the introjector who swallows material that is disgusting to him and should be censored by his taste—could not be solved in that session. We worked a bit on it, but there the patient had a blank, a blind spot. His palate was completely desensitized.

From the foregoing, the reader can see some of the significant differences between Gestalt therapy and the more conventional techniques. But the most important differences, I think, have not yet been discussed explicitly.

4 HERE AND NOW THERAPY

Implicit in the emphasis of orthodox psychotherapy is the point of view that the neurotic is a person who once had a problem, and that the resolution of this past problem is the goal of psychotherapy. The whole approach to treatment through memory and the past indicates this assumption, which runs directly counter to everything we observe about neurosis and the neurotic. From the Gestalt viewpoint the neurotic is not merely a person who once *had* a problem, he is a person who has a *continuing* problem, here and now, in the present. Although it may well be that he is acting the way he is today "because" of things that happened to him in the past, his difficulties today are connected with the ways he is acting today. He cannot get along in the present, and unless he learns how to deal with problems as they arise, he will not be able to get along in the future.

The goal of therapy, then, must be to give him the means with which he can solve his present problems and any that may arise tomorrow or next year. That tool is self-support, and this he achieves by dealing with himself and his problems with all the means presently at his command, right now. If he can become *truly aware* at every instant of himself and his actions on whatever level—fantasy, verbal or physical—he can see how he is producing his difficulties, he can see what his present difficulties are, and he can help himself to solve them in the present, in the here and now. Each one he solves makes easier the solution of the next, for every solution increases his self-support.

If therapy is successful the patient will inevitably

have taken care of the tag ends of his past unsolved problems, because these tag ends are bound to cause trouble in the present, and so they are bound to come up in the course of the therapeutic session, disguised in any number of different ways—disassociations, nervous habits, fantasies, etc. But these tag ends of the past are also current problems which inhibit the patient's participation in the present.

The neurotic is, by accepted definition, a person whose difficulties make his present life unsuccessful. In addition, by our definition, he is a person who chronically engages in self-interruption, who has an inadequate sense of identity (and thus cannot distinguish properly between himself and the rest of the world), who has inadequate means of self-support, whose psychological homeostasis is out of order, and whose behavior arises from misguided efforts in the direction of achieving balance.

Within this general framework, we can see what must be done. The neurotic finds it difficult to participate fully in the present—his past unfinished business gets in his way. His problems exist in the here and now—and yet too often only part of him is here to cope with them. Through therapy, he must learn to live in the present, and his therapeutic sessions must be his first practice at this hitherto unaccomplished task. Gestalt therapy is therefore a "here and now" therapy, in which we ask the patient during the session to turn all his attention to what he is doing at the present, during the course of the session—right here and now.

Gestalt therapy is an experiential therapy, rather than a verbal or an interpretive therapy. We ask our patients not to talk about their traumas and their problems in the removed area of the past tense and memory, but to *re-experience* their problems and their traumas—which are their unfinished situations in the present—in the here and now. If the patient is finally to close the book on his past problems, he must close it in the present. For he must realize that if his past problems were really past, they would no longer be problems—and they certainly would not be present.

In addition, as an experiential therapy, the Gestalt

technique demands of the patient that he experience as much of himself as he can, that he experience himself as fully as he can in the here and now. We ask the patient to become aware of his gestures, of his breathing, of his emotions, of his voice, and of his facial expressions as much as of his pressing thoughts. We know that the more he becomes aware of himself, the more he will learn about what his self is. As he experiences the ways in which he prevents himself from "being" now —the ways in which he interrupts himself—he will also begin to experience the self he has interrupted.

In this process, the therapist is guided by what he observes about the patient. We shall discuss the therapist's role in more detail in a later chapter. Here let it suffice to say that the therapist should be sensitive to the surface the patient presents so that the therapist's broader awareness can become the means by which the patient is enabled to increase his own.

The basic sentence with which we ask our patients to begin therapy, and which we retain throughout its course—not only in words, but in spirit—is the simple phrase: "Now I am aware." The now keeps us in the present and brings home the fact that no experience is ever possible except in the present. And the present, itself, is of course an ever-changing experience. Once the now is used, the patient will easily use the present tense throughout, work on a phenomenological basis and, as I will show later, provide the material of past experience which is required to close the gestalt, to assimilate a memory, to right the organismic balance.

The "I" is used as an antidote to the "it" and develops the patient's sense of responsibility for his feelings, thoughts, and symptoms. The "am" is his existential symbol. It brings home whatever he experiences as part of his being, and, together with his now, of his becoming. He quickly learns that each new "now" is different from the previous one.

The "aware" provides the patient with the sense of his own capacities, and abilities, his own sensoric and motor and intellectual equipment. It is not the conscious—for that is purely mental—it is the experience sifted, as it were, only through the mind and through words. The "aware" provides something in addition to the conscious. Working, as we do, with what the patient has, his present means of manipulation, rather than with what he has not developed or what he has lost, the "aware" gives both therapist and patient the best picture of the patient's present resources. For awareness always takes place in the present. It opens up possibilities for action. Routine and habits are established functions, and any need to change them requires that they should be brought into the focus of awareness afresh. The mere idea of changing them presupposes the possibility of alternative ways of thinking and acting. Without awareness, there is no cognition of choice. Awareness, contact, and present are merely different aspects of one and the same process—self-realization. It is here and now that we become aware of all our choices, from small pathological decisions (is this pencil lying straight enough?) to the existential choice of devotion to a cause or avocation.

How does this "now I am aware," this here and now therapy work in action? Let us take the example of a neurotic whose unfinished business is the unfinished labor of mourning a dead parent. Aware or unaware, such a patient fantasizes that his guiding parent is still around; he acts as if the parent were still alive and conducts his life by outdated directions. To become self-supportive and to participate fully in the present as it is, he has to give up this guidance; he has to part, to say a final good-bye to his progenitor. And to do this successfully, he has to go to the deathbed and face the departure. He has to transform his thoughts about the past into actions in the present which he experiences as if the now were the then. He cannot do it merely by re-recounting the scene, he must re-live it. He must go through and assimilate the interrupted feelings which are mostly of intense grief, but which may have in them elements of triumph or guilt or any number of other things. It is insufficient merely to recall a past incident, one has to *psychodramatically* return to it. Just as talking about oneself is a resistance against experiencing oneself, so the memory of an experience—simply talking about it—leaves it isolated as a deposit of the past—as lacking in life as the ruins of Pompei. You are left with the opportunity to make some clever reconstructions, but you don't bring them back alive. The neurotic's memory is more than simply a hunting ground for the archeologists of man's behavior we call psychoanalysts. It is the uncompleted event, which is still alive and interrupted, waiting to be assimilated and integrated. It is here and now, in the present, that this assimilation must take place.

The psychoanalyst, out of the vast stores of his theoretical knowledge, might explain to the patient: "You are still tied to your mother because you feel guilty about her death. It was something you wished for in childhood and repressed, and when your wish came true, you felt like a murderer." And there may be elements of truth in what he says. But this kind of symbolic or intellectual explanation does not affect the patient's feelings, for these are the result not of his sense of guilt, but of his interruption of it when his mother died. If he had permitted himself fully to experience his guilt then, he would not feel distressed now. In Gestalt therapy we therefore require that the patient psychodramatically talk to his dead mother.

Because the neurotic finds it difficult to live and experience himself in the present, he will find it difficult to stick to the here and now technique. He will interrupt his present participation with memories of the past, and he will persist in talking about them as if they were indeed past. He finds it less difficult to associate than to concentrate and, in concentrating, to experience himself. Whether concentrating on his body sensations or his fantasies—although at first he will find this a miserable task—his unfinished business makes concentration a major project for him. He no longer has a clear sense of the order of his needs—he tends to give them all equal value. He is like the young man Stephen Leacock once spoke about who got on his horse and galloped off madly in all directions.

It is not a desire to make his life miserable that lies behind our request to make him capable of concentration. If he is to move towards full participation in the present, to take the first step towards productive living, he must learn to direct his energies—that is, to concentrate. He will be able to move from "now I need this" to "now I need that," only if he truly experiences each now and each need.

In addition, the concentration technique (focal awareness) provides us with a tool for therapy in depth, rather than in breadth. By concentrating on each symptom, each area of awareness, the patient learns several things about himself and his neurosis. He learns what he is actually experiencing. He learns how he experiences it. And he learns how his feelings and behavior in one area are related to his feelings and behavior in other areas.

Let me return for a moment to that classical psychosomatic manifestation, the headache. Patients frequently list this as one of their most annoying symptoms. They complain that their headaches bother them and now, when they come for treatment, they want to bother us with their symptoms. They are, of course, welcome to do so. But we in turn bother them—we ask them to take more responsibility and less aspirin. We do this by asking them to discover through experiencing how they produce their headaches. (The "aha" experience of discovery is one of the most powerful agents for cure.) We ask them first to localize the pain and to stay, or sit, or lie with the tension. We ask them to concentrate on the pain, not to dispose of it. In the beginning only a few will be able to stand the tension. Most patients will tend to interrupt immediately with explanations, associations, or by pooh poohing what we are doing. Consequently, the therapist has to work through one way of interrupting after another, and he has to change these interruptions into "I" functions. This means that even before we work on the headache itself, we have already done a considerable amount of integration. Suppose, for example, the therapist asks the patient to stay with his pains and the patient says, as often happens, "this is all nonsense." If he learns to say, instead, "what you are trying to do is all nonsense," he is taking a tiny step forward. With such a small step we have transformed a minute particle of "it" into a *contact function,* into a self-expression. We might even follow up his statement and ask the patient to elaborate on it. This would give him an opportunity to come out with a lot of his unspoken skepticism, distrust, and so on, and all of these are part of the unfinished businesses that are preventing his total participation in the present.

But finally the patient will be able to stay with his headache, and with his pains, which he can now localize. This staying with is opening up the possibility for development of contact with the self. If he stays with his pains he may find that he has been contracting some muscles or that he feels a numbness. Let us say that he discovers his pains are associated with muscle contractions. Then we will ask him to exaggerate the contracting. He will then see how he can voluntarily create and intensify his own pains. He might then say, as a result of his discoveries up to now, "It's as if I were screwing up my face to cry." The therapist might then ask, "Would you like to cry?" And then, if we ask him to direct that remark directly to us, to say it to our face, he might well burst out crying and weeping. "I won't cry, damn you! Leave me alone, leave me alone!" Apparently, then, his headache was an interruption of the need to cry. It has become apparent that he has lost his need to interrupt his crying by giving himself headaches. At best, the patient may lose his need to cry, too, for if the therapy can be concentrated on this one factor for a long enough period of time, he may be able to work through the past interruptions that also led to the need to cry in the present. But even before this stage, progress has been made. The patient has transformed a partial involvement (headache) into a total involvement (weeping). He has transformed a psychosomatic symptom into an expression of the total self, because in his short outburst of despair he was wholly and totally involved. So through the concentration technique the patient has learned how to participate fully in at least one present experience. He has learned at the same time something about his process of self-interruption and the ways in which these self-interruptions are related to the totality of his experience. He has discovered one of his means of manipulation.

The neurotic is, as we said, a self-interrupter. All

schools of psychotherapy take this fact into account. Freud, as a matter of fact, built his therapy around a recognition of this phenomenon. Of all the possible forms of self-interruption he chose a very decisive one, which he called the Censor. He said, "Do not interrupt the free flow of your associations." But he also assumed that the Censor was the servant of embarrassment, and thus spoke Freud: "Do not be embarrassed." Precisely with these two taboos he interrupted the patient's experience of his embarrassment and his experience of its dissolution. This results in a desensitization, an inability to experience embarrassment, or even (and this applies still more to patients in Reichian therapy) in overcompensating brazenness. What has to be tackled in therapy is not the censored material but the censoring itself, the form that self-interruption takes. Again, we cannot work from the inside out, but only from the outside in.

The therapeutic procedure (which is the re-establishment of the self by integrating the dissociated parts of the personality) must bring the patient to the point where he no longer interrupts himself, that is, to the point where he is no longer neurotic. How can we do this without making the mistake of interrupting the interruption? We have previously mentioned Freud's command, "do not censor," which is in itself a censoring of the censor, an interruption of the process of censoring. What we have to do is notice and deal with the *hows* of every interruption, rather than with the censor —which is Freud's postulated *why* of interruption. If we deal with the interruptions per se, we deal with the direct clinical picture, with the experience the patient is living through. Again, we deal with the surface that presents itself. There is no need to guess and to interpret. We hear the interruption of a sentence or we notice that the patient holds his breath or we see that he is making a fist, as if to hit someone, or swinging his legs as if to kick, or we observe how he interrupts contact with the therapist by looking away.

Is he aware of these self-interruptions? This must be our first question to him in such a situation. Does he know that this is what he is doing? As he becomes more aware of the ways in which he interrupts himself, he will inevitably become more aware of what he is interrupting. As our example of the headache showed, it was in staying with his interruption, his headache, that he discovered how he was using this mechanism to interrupt his own crying. This example shows how, by concentrating on the interruption per se—on the hows of it, not its whys—the patient comes to an awareness of the fact that he is interrupting himself, and becomes aware of what he is interrupting. He also becomes able to dissolve his interruptions and to live through and finish up one unfinished experience.

The neurotic mechanisms of introjection, projection, and retroflection are themselves mechanisms of introjection, and often developed in response to interruptions from the outside world. In the normal process of growth, we learn through trial and error, through testing our lives and our world as freely and uninterruptedly as possible.

Imagine a kitten climbing a tree. It is engaged in experimenting. It balances itself, it tests its strength and its agility. But the mother cat will not leave it alone; she insists that it come down. "You may break your neck, you naughty kitten," she hisses. How this would interrupt the kitten's pleasure in growing! It would even interrupt the growth process itself. But cats, of course, do not behave so stupidly. They leave the pursuit of safety to the human beings.

On the contrary, the cat, like any other animal and any sensible human being, will consider it the essence of up-bringing to facilitate the transformation of external into self-support. The newly born kitten can neither feed, transport, nor defend itself. For all this it needs its mother. But it will develop the means to do these things itself, partly through developing its inborn instincts, and partly through environmental teaching. In the human being, the transition from external to self-support is, of course, more complicated. Consider only the need to change diapers, to dress, to cook, to choose a vocation, or to gain knowledge.

Since we are forced to learn so much more through education than by using our inherited instincts, much of the animal's intuition as to what is the right procedure is missing. Instead, the "right" procedure is established by composite fantasies which are handed over and modified from generation to generation. They are mostly support functions for social contact, such as manners and codes of behavior (ethics), means of orientation (reading, weltanschauungen), standards of beauty (aesthetics), and social position (attitudes). Often, however, these procedures are not biologically oriented, thus disrupting the very root of our existence and leading to degeneration. Psychiatric case histories show over and over how our depreciatory orientation towards sex can produce neurosis. But whether these procedures are anti-biological or anti-personal or anti-social, they are interruptions in the on-going processes which, if left alone, would lead to self-support.

Such interruptions are the nightmares of Junior's upbringing. There are the *interruptions of contact*, the "don't touch that!" and the "don't do that!" that fly around his ears day in and day out. Or "leave me alone! Can't I have a moment's peace," interrupt his wish to interrupt mamma. His *withdrawals* are also interrupted. "You stay here now, keep your mind on your homework and don't dream," or "you can't go out to play until you finish your dinner."

Shall we then follow a policy of utter non-interruption? Like any other animal, Junior has to test the world, to find his possibilities, to try to expand his boundaries, to experiment with how far he can go. But at the same time he has to be prevented from doing serious harm to himself or others. He has to learn to cope with interruptions.

The real trouble begins when the parents interfere with the child's maturation, either by spoiling him and interrupting his attempts to find his own bearings or by being overprotective, and destroying his confidence in his ability to be self-supportive within the limits of his development. They regard the child as a possession to be either preserved or exhibited. In the latter case, they will tend to create precocity by making ambitious demands on the child, who at that time lacks sufficient inner support to fulfill them. In the former case, they will tend to block maturation by giving the child no chance to make use of the inner supports he has developed. The first child may grow up self-sufficient, the second dependent—neither self-supportive.

Our patients come to us having incorporated their parents' interruptions into their own lives—and this is introjection. Such patients are the ones who say to us, for example, "grown men don't cry!" They come to us having disowned the offending parts of themselves—the ones that were interrupted in their childhood—this is projection. "These darn headaches! Why do I have to suffer from them!" They may turn the qualities their parents called bad, and the display of which they interrupted, against themselves. This is retroflection. "I must control myself. I must not let myself cry!" They may have become so confused by their parents' interruptions that they give up their identity completely and forget the difference and the connection between their internal needs and the external means of satisfying them. This result is confluence. "I always get a headache when people yell at me."

Through making our patients aware, in the here and now, by concentration, of what these interruptions are, of how these interruptions affect them, we can bring them to real integrations. We can dissolve the endless clinch in which they find themselves. We can give them a chance to be themselves, because they will begin to experience themselves; this will give them a true appreciation both of themselves and others, and will enable them to make good contact with the world, because they will know where the world is. Understanding means, basically, seeing a part in its relation to the whole. For our patients, it means seeing themselves as part of the total field and thus becoming related both to themselves and to the world. This is good contact.

5 PEELING THE ONION

Questions are o.k.

We can now go on to a more extended discussion of techniques and results. First of all, we would like to make explicit certain observations which themselves form a large part of the rationale behind our procedure.

In the "Now I am aware" experiment, discussed in the fourth chapter, the patient's area of awareness is usually limited to external sensory impressions when he first tries it. Later, it broadens to include many other factors, internal as well as external, as he continues. In other words, simply becoming aware that you are aware increases your potential area of operation. It gives a wider orientation and greater freedom of choice and action.

This fact is extremely important for the neurotic. As I pointed out earlier, he does not lack the ability to manipulate his environment, but he does very definitely lack an orientation within it. He is boxed in by his unawareness both of himself and of the external situation and has very little room in which to maneuver. But as soon as his awareness is increased, his orientation and his maneuverability are also increased. He is then in better contact since contact requires orientation to the moment.

This is important for the neurotic. He has little sense of self; he is always interrupting his self. It only rarely gets through to him. Consequently, he cannot easily express himself. Even this rudimentary and rather simple way of expression is a great step forward.

I am convinced that the awareness technique alone can produce valuable therapeutic results. If the therapist were limited in his work only to asking three questions, he would eventually achieve success with all but the most seriously disturbed of his patients. These three questions, which are essentially reformulations of the statement, "Now I am aware" are: "What are you doing?" "What do you feel?" "What do you want?" We could increase the number by two, and include these questions: "What do you avoid?" "What do you expect?" These are obviously extensions of the first three. And they would be enough of an armamentarium for the therapist.

All five of these are healthily supportive questions. That is, the patient can only answer them to the degree that his own awareness makes possible. But at the same time, they help him to become more aware. They throw him on his own resources, bring him to a recognition of his own responsibility, ask him to muster his forces and his means of self-support. They give him a sense of self because they are directed to his self.

His verbal answers to them may come from the intellect, but his total response, unless he is completely desensitized, comes from his total person and is an indication of his total personality. Aside from the pat answers which are always readily available to him there will nearly always be some additional reaction—a confusion, a hesitation, a knitting of the brow, a shrug of the shoulder, a suppressed "what a silly question!" a bit of embarrassment, a wish not to be bothered, an "oh, gosh, here he goes again," an eager leaning forward, and so on. Each of these responses is many times more important than the verbal answer. Each one of them is an indication of the self and of the patient's style. At first the patient's behavior may be of more value to the therapist than it is to him. The therapist, having a wider area of awareness, can see the behavior as a function of the total personality. The patient, whose awareness is still limited, may be completely oblivious to anything but his verbal answer. Or, if he is not oblivious, he may be unable to grasp the significance of his style of response. But eventually there will be a click in the patient's awareness, too. This will be the first big step he makes in therapy.

The therapist can help the patient to this self-discovery by acting, as it were, as a magnifying mirror for him. The therapist cannot make discoveries for the patient, he can only facilitate the process in the patient. By his questions he can bring the patient to see his own behavior more clearly and he can help the patient determine for himself what that behavior represents.

And the acute therapist can find plenty of material right under his nose; he needs only to look. Unfortunately, even this is not so easy, for to look and to see requires that the therapist be completely empty and unbiased. Since *contact always occurs on the surface,* it is the surface that the therapist must see. But make no mistake about it, that surface is much broader and more significant than the orthodox therapist will admit. First of all, their preconvictions prevent them from seeing much of it. And second of all, they tend to take it for granted, to talk about it contemptuously as "obvious." This is where they make their biggest mistake. As long as we take anything for granted and dismiss it as obvious we have not the slightest inclination to make a change nor do we have the tools with which to do it.

But consider for a moment this fact: everything the patient does, obvious or concealed, is an expression of the self. His leaning forward and pushing back, his abortive kicks, his fidgets, his subtleties of enunciation, his split-second hesitations between words, his handwriting, his use of metaphor and language, his use of "it" as opposed to his use of "you" and "I"; all are on the surface, all are obvious, and all are meaningful. These are the only real material the therapist has to work with. His preconvictions will not help the patient at all.

The therapist's questions, then, will be based on his observations and directed towards bringing certain factors within the area of the patient's awareness. He uses the technique of asking questions rather than of making statements so that the burden of recognition and action is placed where it belongs—on the patient. But his questions are actually translations of his observations. Such as: "Are you aware of your speech?" might represent the following observation and might be turned into the following statement: "I am aware that you speak extremely rapidly. I also notice that you are continuously short of breath. It would be beneficial to you to become aware yourself of what you are doing so that we can cope with the excitement you are dissipating in this way."

There is, however, one way of asking questions—used by most orthodox therapists—which seems to me of little therapeutic value. These are the questions starting with "why?" I have discussed this somewhat before, but the subject seems to me to be of sufficient importance to return to it again.

The "why" questions produce only pat answers, defensiveness, rationalizations, excuses, and the delusion that an event can be explained by a single cause. The why does not discriminate purpose, origin, or background. Under the mask of inquiry it has contributed perhaps more to human confusion than any other single word. Not so with the "how." The how inquires into the structure of an event, and once the structure is clear all the whys are automatically answered. Once we have clarified the structure of the headache we can answer all the questions of the whys-guys ad libitum. Our patient had headaches "because" he suppressed his crying, "because" he did not express himself, "because" he contracted his muscles, "because" he interrupted himself, "because" he had introjected a command not to cry, and so on. If we spend our time looking for causes instead of structure we may as well give up the idea of therapy and join the group of worrying grandmothers who attack their prey with such pointless questions as "Why did you catch that cold?" "Why have you been so naughty?"

Of course, all of the therapist's questions are interruptions of some on-going process in the patient. They are intrusions, very often miniature shocks. This leads to an apparently unfair situation. If the therapist has to frustrate the demands of the patient but feels himself free to fire questions, is this not an unfair situation, an authoritarian procedure, completely antithetical to our effort to elevate the therapist from the position of a power figure to a human being? Admittedly, it is not easy to find the way through this inconsistency, but once the therapist has resolved the psychotherapeutic paradox of working with *support* and *frustration* both, his procedures will fall correctly into place.

The therapist is not, of course, the only one who can ask questions. And it is impossible to enumerate the many things the patient can do with this technique. His questions can be intelligent and therapy-supporting. They can be irritating and repetitious. They can be the "what did you says" and the "what do you means" of the semantically blocked. Nor is it always apparent from which area of confusion the patient's questions arise. Sometimes he does not know whether he can trust the therapist, so he will use questions to test him. If he has obsessional doubts, he will ask the same question over and over again.

The majority of questions the patient asks are seductions of the intellect, related to the notion that verbal explanations are a substitute for understanding. As long as such patients are fed with interpretations, especially if they are emotionally blocked, they'll snuggle happily back in the cocoon of their neurosis and stay there, purring peacefully.

The idea of frustrating the patient's questions is as old as psychotherapy itself. Even such a simple response as "why do you ask this question?" is meant to throw the patient back on his own resources. But, as previously pointed out, the why question is a very inadequate tool. We want to elicit the structure of the patient's question, its background; and possibly we can reach the self in this process. And so our technique is to ask our patients to turn their questions into propositions or statements.

At first they will merely circumscribe the questions in other words but stick to the questioning—"I am curious . . ." Then we repeat our request. Now the patient might say, "I am of this or that opinion; what do you think?" This is at least one step forward—now the patient displays to himself his unsureness and his need for intellectual support. We can go further and ask for another reformulation, and then the patient may loosen up and a lot of material that has been held back may be released. Take this example:

Patient: What do you mean by support?
Therapist: Could you turn that into a statement?
Patient: I would like to know what you mean by support.
Therapist: That's still a question. Could you turn it into a statement?
Patient: I would like to tear hell out of you on this question if I had the opportunity.

Now we have a direct bit of self-expression. True, it is hostile, but socially inacceptable as it may be, it gives the patient a tiny bit of increased self-support by giving him an increased self-awareness. Although the therapist could get along with the five questions mentioned early in the chapter, he does not limit himself to these. For as the therapist's initial awareness questions are a way of getting through to the patient's self, so the patient's statements and ways of manipulating the therapist give us clues as to the neurotic mechanisms through which he is shoring himself up against what he considers to be existential collapse. The patient's statements are always clues for further questions, and possibly more specific ones.

What the patient does through these mechanisms is, in essence, to shirk responsibility for his behavior. To him responsibility is blame, and as afraid as he is of being blamed, so is he ready to blame. "I'm not responsible for my attitudes, it's my neurosis that's at fault," he seems to be saying. But responsibility is really response-ability, the ability to choose one's reactions. Whether the neurotic dissociates himself from himself through projection, introjection, confluence or retroflection, he is in a position where, having abdicated responsibility he has also given up his response-ability and his freedom of choice.

To reintegrate the neurotic we have to make use of whatever share of responsibility he is willing to take. The same thing applies to the therapist. He has to take full responsibility for his reactions to the patient. He is not responsible for the patient's neurosis, nor for his misery or misunderstandings, but he is responsible for his own motives and his handling of the patient and the therapeutic situation.

The therapist's primary responsibility is not to let go unchallenged any statement or behavior which is not representative of the self, which is evidence of the patient's lack of self-responsibility. This means that he must deal with each one of the neurotic mechanisms as it appears. Each one must be integrated by the patient and must be transformed into an expression of self so that he can truly discover his self.

How do we deal with these mechanisms? The examples given earlier of the crying-headache and the gasping-anxiety attack indicate some of the ways we can work with confluences. Both of these psychosomatic symptoms are, in essence, evidence of confluence. The victims have locked control of the muscles around their eyes with control of the need to cry in the first case and have locked control of their breathing with control of their emotional responses in the second. Having established an identity between two different terms of two different relationships, they interrupt the second term of each one by interrupting the first. We help the patient dissolve the clinch by helping him discover, through his experience of the symptom, how he has artificially connected the two together, substituting the symptom for the self-expression and self-experience.

What are the evidences of retroflection? These we find often in the patient's physical behavior as well as in his use of the "myself" language. For example, suppose that the patient is sitting talking about something and we notice that he is punching one of his palms with his other fist. This is, fairly obviously, retroflective behavior. If the therapist asks him, "Whom would you like to punch?" the patient may at first look at the therapist in bewilderment—"Oh, that's just a nervous habit." In other words, for this behavior, at this point, he is not willing to take responsibility. But as therapy continues and the patient's area of awareness broadens, his responsibility will broaden, too. If the nervous habit continues, the patient will one day, in response to the therapist's question, give a direct answer that comes from the self. It may be "my mother," or "my father," or "my boss," or "you." Whatever it is, the patient will at this point have become aware of his behavior, of its object, and of his self. We do not leave the situation there, of course, but I do not want here to describe further ways of handling it. They will be discussed in general in the next chapter.

It is very often startling to someone who has had limited experience with Gestalt therapy to see how quickly, how clearly, and how smoothly the response is made. It is almost as if the patient has been waiting desperately for a chance to express himself. It is startling not only to the observer, but often to the patient himself.

When the patient makes a statement that seems to the therapist to be a projection, we can handle it by asking the patient to do one of several things. If he has been talking in "it" terms—"it bothers me," as with the headache, we have to get him first to associate himself with his headache. This he does by seeing how he produces his headaches so that the headache is no longer an it but a part of him. If he expresses opinions of others which are projections, "they don't like me," "they're always trying to push me around," we ask him to reverse the statement. "I don't like them," or "I'm always trying to push people around," and we may have him continue repeating it until it emerges as a felt self-expression.

We can deal with introjection in just the opposite way by making the patient aware of his attitude towards the introjected material. It is interesting to see how quickly the emotional awareness of swallowing whole can turn into actual physical nausea and the desire to throw up.

Often we will request the patient to try an experiment, the material for which has been provided by our observation of him—either what he does or what he does not do. The purpose of the experiment is to help the patient find out for himself how he interrupts himself and prevents himself from succeeding. The goals in our therapeutic experiments are not likely to be reached. Whatever the patient can do to manipulate the therapist remains strong, but the patient will not be content to leave the situation at that. He will go on and on, always meeting tolerable frustration, until the time comes when he becomes aware of what he is doing.

If, on the other hand, the patient is genuinely blocked, he will show signs of this, too. He may blush or stammer. Now we continue our experiment in fantasy, since the patient cannot begin as yet to carry it out in either the real or the playacting levels.

Therapist: If you said it, could you imagine what my response would be?

Patient: Yes, you will think "what a horrible creature you are."

Therapist: Could you imagine a situation where you could say to me, "what a horrible creature you are?"

Patient: (In an animated voice) Yes, that's exactly what I thought. What a horrible creature you are to put me in such an embarrassing position.

Therapist: Could you give me more details as to how I like to put people into embarrassing positions?

The patient is now freer than he was. And he may be ready to do some psychodrama in fantasy about how someone makes people embarrassed, thereby changing one more projection (the therapist wants to embarrass me) into self-expression. By the time the session is over, the patient might realize that he interrupts the pleasure he gets from embarrassing others by being embarrassed himself.

We have now internalized the projected conflict and we can easily integrate its two components: to interrupt and to embarrass. We might find, for example, that the patient feels that by stopping me in my therapeutic endeavors he would embarrass me. In this way, he would control me and make me feel helpless. Obviously we have here an attitude which, if not quickly uncovered, would sabotage the whole treatment. So we suggest that he fantasize about his need to control people. We might find wild fantasies about crushing people so that they cannot hurt him. Now we can internalize the projected hurting and integrate to crush and to hurt, as before we integrated interruption and embarrassment.

At this point the therapist will probably notice that the patient is beginning to use his muscles; perhaps he makes a fist or there is some sudden movement of the arm or leg. Now more of his total personality is involved in his self-expression. While before he might have been rigid from the elbow up, now he is, for the first time, moving his shoulders. Instead of feeling crushed, as he so often does, he might now feel like crushing, which means that he is taking the first step towards manual and dental aggression, towards destructuring and assimilating.

Although this account is oversimplified, it shows three important things: The therapist can always work with the events present, either in physical actuality or in fantasy. Secondly, he can integrate immediately whatever comes up in the course of the session and does not have to let the unfinished situations accumulate. And finally, the therapist can work with experiences, and not only with verbalizations or memories. As a matter of fact, there is hardly a patient in Gestalt therapy who does not tell us that he has more experiences in the first few sessions of our therapy than he had in many months of analysis. Even if we make allowances for the patients' need to manipulate the therapist with flattery, these remarks are made too regularly to be disregarded.

There is one problem in Gestalt therapy which exists in all other therapies too. That is, that the patient adjusts himself to our technique. Then he may start to manipulate the therapist with manufactured and irrelevant experiences just to please him and at the same time avoid coping with his own difficulties. Then the accent in therapy has to shift from having experiences to faking them, and the therapist has to cope with the patient's "let's pretend" attitude.

We ask all our patients to try doing some homework, and many are capable of speeding up their therapy considerably in this way. All of them, of course, are full of good intentions when the request is made, and all of them promise to do their assignments faithfully, but a good number of them fail. As soon as they come close to the danger zone—and the awareness technique has been developed for just this purpose—they detour themselves in one way or another.

Theoretically this homework is so simple that it seems incredible that the patient should go to such great lengths to avoid it. It is, after all, a considerable saving of time and money. But although the neurotic wants to be "cured," he also feels safer and better-dressed with his neurosis than without it, and he is afraid that successful therapy will hurl him into a bottomless pit. He would rather bear those ills he has than fly to others that he knows not of. But eventually, as therapy progresses and the patient develops more areas of self-support, he becomes more able to cope with his homework.

The homework consists of reviewing the session in terms of a systematic application of the awareness technique. A review of some sort is bound to occur in every kind of therapy. Some patients will remember a few interesting points in the session, some will react to the session—they will be pleased, resentful, pondering, depressed. Others will forget what has happened as soon as they leave the consulting room.

What we ask the patient to do, in line with our entire approach, is to imagine himself back in the consulting room. What does he experience? Can he go over the entire session without difficulty? Can he find blanks? If so, is he aware of these blanks—that is, does he feel there was something vaguely disturbing that he cannot put his finger on? Did he express everything there was to be expressed towards the therapist? Can he do it now and can he do it with his whole self? Can he become aware of avoiding and interrupting any of the aspects of the total expression—in other words, is he preponderantly involved with his emotions or his movements or his sensations or his visualizations or his verbalizations? Does he say what he feels and does he feel what he says?

The examples I have given and the techniques I have outlined may seem rather mundane and undramatic, as contrasted with the archaeological expeditions in orthodox analysis, which one day recover the castration complex, the next day dig up the remnants of the Oedipal situation, the third day recall all the traumatic events of the primal scene. But in fact the emotional charge in each session of Gestalt therapy, no matter how mundane its subject matter, is extremely high. If emotion is, as I have hypothesized, the basic force that energizes all action, it exists in every life situation. One of the most serious problems of modern man is that he has desensitized himself to all but the most overwhelming kind of emotional response. To the degree that he is no longer capable of feeling sensitively, to that degree he becomes incapable of the freedom of choice that results in a relevant action.

No, there is nothing foolish or wasteful or petty about our method of getting at problems. Since the aim of therapy is to give the patient a tool—self-support—with which he can solve his own difficulties, we can work effectively with each situation as it presents itself. We can open one door at a time and peel off one layer of the onion at a time. Each layer is part of the neurosis, as it is dealt with it changes the problem, as the problems change, so the specifics are changed. At each step of the way, since the patient's self-support has been increased a trifle in each session, the next step becomes easier to take.

6 SHUTTLING, PSYCHODRAMA, AND CONFUSION

There is one obvious limitation to the awareness technique used alone. It would probably take years to achieve its results, as do most of the orthodox therapies, and at that rate, psychiatry could never catch up with the constantly increasing number of people who are mentally disturbed and the still more rapidly increasing number of people who live far below their potentials. Although the analytical approach has failed to provide us with a tool that can cope with the social emergency, the awareness technique by itself would be equally limited.

But, having recognized the relationship between fantasy and actuality, we can make full use in therapy of fantasizing and all its increasing states of intensity towards actuality—a verbalized fantasy, or one which is written down, or one which is acted out as psychodrama. We can play at psychodrama with our patients, or we can ask them to play at this game alone, a game which we term "monotherapy."

In this latter case, the patient creates his own stage, his own actors, his own props, direction and expression. This gives him a chance to realize that everything he fantasizes is his, and gives him a chance to see the conflicts inside him. Monotherapy thus avoids the contamination, the precepts of others which are usually present in ordinary psychodrama.

We make use of several other techniques as well. The first I would like to discuss is the shuttle technique. As an approach, it is nothing new. The Freudians handle dreams in precisely this way, by asking the patient to shuttle between the manifest content of a dream and its associations. But the systematic application of the technique in Gestalt therapy and the particular way in which it is applied are both new. I have already demonstrated its use in our experiment on acute anxiety, in which I asked the patient to shuttle his attention from his breathing to his muscles, from his muscles to his breathing, until the relationship between the two becomes clear and the patient can breathe freely. This shuttling helps us to break up patterns of confluence, such as we see in the headache that turns out to be a disguised crying.

One of my first "miracle" cures was due to an intuitive application of this technique. A young man came for therapy whose major complaint was sexual impotence. He told me in great detail about his background, family situation, social activities, etc. But what was most interesting was his remark that although his health in general was good, he was under treatment by an ear-nose-and-throat specialist for chronic nasal congestion. This struck me as the most vital clue to his problem, and remembering the Fleiss-Freud observation that swelling of the nasal mucous membrane was often a displacement from the genital area, I asked him if he would be willing to stop medical treatment temporarily. He agreed. During his next session, I requested him to direct his concentration alternately to his nasal sensations and his non-existent genital sensations. And an extraordinary thing happened. The nasal swelling decreased and the tumescence of the penis increased. Now he could both breathe freely and have sexual relations. He had not only interrupted his penis erections and displaced both the sensation and the tumescence to his nose, he had even begun to compartmentalize his symptoms and to pander to his dissociations by having different specialists attend to them. While the ear-nose-and-throat doctor was used to working on dissociated symptoms and local "causes," the Gestalt approach enabled me to look for the total situation, to examine the structure of the field, to see the problem in its total context and to treat it in a unified way.

When we look at displacements in this way, it becomes evident that they cannot be dealt with where they occur because they have no functional meaning in that place. The displacement must be brought back to where it belongs; it can only be resolved in the area where it has meaning. The patient who suffers from pains in the eyes which are due to the retention of tears, can dissolve his pains only in crying. The patient who has displaced from the testicles (in the vernacular, the balls) where there is retained semen—to the eyeballs (and I have had several such patients) will have to shift his pains back to where they belong before they can be dealt with. Not until then can he enjoy a good orgasm and lose his symptoms.

Now let me present another example, less dramatic but equally valid. Here we shuttle, not as the orthodox analyst does, between memory and associations, but between the reliving of a memory and the here and now. As I have previously mentioned, we treat all time during the therapeutic session as if it were here and now; for awareness and experience can only take place in the present. But even with the most vivid visualization and reliving of a memory, the knowledge that it is something from the past remains in the background. This is not true, however, with what we call the proprioceptions—the internal, muscular kinesthetic sense. The proprioceptions are timeless, and can only be experienced as here and now. Thus, if we shuttle between visualization and proprioception we will be able to fill in the blanks and complete the unfinished business of the past. The trained therapist will also take into account any involuntary movements the patient makes—shrugging his shoulders, kicking his feet, etc., and draw the patient's attention to them.

Suppose the patient has fantasized a return to a recent experience which bothered him. The first thing he says when he comes into the consulting room is that his job is getting on his nerves. Nobody, he says, treats him with enough respect. There isn't anything special that he can put his finger on, but the whole atmosphere is distasteful to him. Little things get him down. Something very unimportant happened in the company restaurant that very day. It disturbed him, and he cannot understand why he should have been so upset by it.

We ask him to return, in fantasy, to the experience that bothered him. This is what might happen:

Patient: I am sitting in our cafeteria. My boss is eating a few tables away.

Therapist: What do you feel?

Patient: Nothing. He is talking to someone. Now he is getting up.

Therapist: What do you feel now?

Patient: My heart is pounding. He is moving towards me. Now I am getting excited. He is passing me.

Therapist: What do you feel now?

Patient: Nothing. Absolutely nothing.

Therapist: Are you aware that you are making a fist?

Patient: No. Now that you mention it, though, I feel it. As a matter of fact, I was angry that the boss passed right by me but talked to someone else whom I dislike very much. I was angry at myself for being so touchy.

Therapist: Were you angry with anybody else, too?

Patient: Sure. With that guy the boss stopped to talk to. What right has he got to disturb the boss? See—my arm is shaking. I could hit him right now, the dirty apple-polisher.

We can now take the next step and shuttle between the patient's feelings and his projections. Still better, we could go over the scene again. The phrase "apple-polisher" makes us suspicious. Perhaps the patient was not angry with the boss when he felt the short pang of excitement or anxiety early in the scene.

Therapist: Let's go back to the moment when your boss gets up from the table. What do you feel when you visualize that?

Patient: Wait a minute . . . He is getting up. He is coming towards me. I am getting excited; I hope he will talk to me. I feel myself getting warm in the face. Now he is passing me. I feel very disappointed.

This was a minor traumatic situation for the patient.

The excitement that was mobilized when the boss appeared could not find appropriate expression and the positive cathexis towards the boss (I hope he will talk to me) changed into a negative one—towards the patient's competitor. This negative cathexis, it later turned out, was actually directed towards the patient's projections, from experiencing and satisfying his own needs and desires.

The new patient usually finds considerable initial difficulty in working with the shuttle technique to recover missing abstractions. But with time it becomes easier, and it brings important rewards. Some patients, for example, never listen; others have no emotions to speak of; still others cannot verbalize; yet a fourth group has no power of self-expression at all. Let's work a bit on the theoretically simplest problem—the inability to express oneself.

Take the case of a fairly successful middle-aged man who seems to be in need of a wailing wall. He will start out by complaining to the therapist no end about his wife, his children, his employees, his competitors, etc. But we do not let him continue this indirect expression. We ask him either to visualize himself talking to them or, psychodramatically, to talk to the therapist as if he were the offending wife, children, or whatever. As is our usual practice, we make it clear to him that he should not force himself to succeed—he should not interrupt himself. We make it clear to him that our experiments are carried out for the purpose of making him more aware of the ways in which he is blocking himself, and that what we want him to do is to convert the blocked areas, or repressions, into expressions.

In such a situation we actually have three positions among which to shuttle: the patient's complaining (his manipulation of the therapist for support), his inadequate self-expression (which is a lack of good contact and self-support), and his inhibitions (which are the patient's self-interruptions). The following is the kind of thing that might happen:

Patient: My wife has no consideration for me. (This is a complaint, one of his techniques of manipulating the outside world to give him the support he cannot give himself.)

Therapist: Can you imagine telling this to her face? (We are asking him here not to call on us for support, but to express himself directly.)

Patient: No, I can't. She'd interrupt me as soon as I began. (A complaint again.)

Therapist: Could you tell her that? (Again a request that he express himself directly.)

Patient: Yes. You never let me talk. (This is still a complaint, but at least it is direct. The therapist notes that the soft voice in which the patient uttered it belies his words.)

Therapist: Can you hear your voice? (Here we have shuttled from the complaint to the inadequate means of self-expression.)

Patient: Yes. Sounds rather weak, doesn't it? (A self-interruption.)

Therapist: Could you give an order—something starting with the words "you should"? (In other words, the therapist is asking the patient to express himself simply, directly, and appropriately.)

Patient: No, I could not.

Therapist: What do you feel now? (Here we shuttle to the sensations that accompany the patient's actions.)

Patient: My heart is beating. I am getting anxious.

Therapist: Could you tell this to your wife?

Patient: No. But I'm getting angry. I feel like saying, "shut up for once." (And now we have something more than complaining, self-interrupting, and inexpressiveness. We have an indirect self-expression.)

Therapist: You just said it to her.

Patient: (Shouting) Shut up, shut up! SHUT UP!! For heaven's sake, let me get a word in. (Explosive self-expression.)

The therapist says nothing; the patient is now on his way alone. And very soon he says: "No, I could not say 'shut up' to her, but now I can imagine interrupting her." And he begins to play-act that interruption: "Please, let me say something."

How far can we permit this acting to go? For acting out his neurotic tendencies is often harmful to the patient. Freud saw this and warned against the danger of acting out in daily life, outside the consulting room. He wanted the patient to keep in mind the neurotic tendency he was repeating. Our emphasis is a little different. We say that we want the patient to become aware, in the consulting room, of the meaning of what he is doing. And we believe that he can achieve this awareness by acting out—in therapy, on the fantasy level—whatever there is to be completed. This, as a matter of fact, is the basic concept of Gestalt therapy. The patient feels compelled to repeat in daily life everything that he cannot bring to a satisfactory conclusion. These repetitions are his unfinished business. But he cannot come to a creative solution in this way because he brings his interruptions along with his repetitions, his acting-out. Thus, if he is acting out a neurotic tendency in his extra-therapeutic life, we ask him, during his sessions, to repeat deliberately in fantasy what he has been doing in actuality. In this way we can uncover the moment at which he interrupts the flow of experiences and thus prevents himself from coming to a creative solution.

Let's take an example almost directly opposite the one we described before. Our patient has difficulties with his wife which are unquestionably related to the fact that he is acting out his neurotic tendencies in every-day life. As therapy progresses he becomes more and more aware that there are many things he would like to say to her which he will not express; they would hurt her. But he still has not come to a creative solution, and he interrupts his direct expression by being indirectly sadistic. He is consistently late for dinner, he ignores her, in general he behaves in a manner calculated to be irritating. If we ask him to act out in therapy what he cannot do in reality, to remove his interruptions and fantasize and express in her absence what he would say in her presence, were he not afraid, we will find initially the same reluctance to talk to her in fantasy as we find in actuality. But as the reluctance diminishes, and the patient is able to express—to the therapist, as if the therapist were his wife—more and more of his resentments, he will learn how to cope with them and he will have no need to return to his indirect sadism.

There are other patients who simply don't listen. They may drown the therapist with words. They may interrupt him. They may look attentive, but it is obvious that anything the therapist says goes in one ear and out the other. They may literally not hear him. They may misinterpret his requests and his statements. We let these patients shuttle between talking and listening to themselves. At first we ask them, after each of their sentences: "Are you aware of this sentence?" They usually remember having said the words, but they often say that they were not aware of them as they spoke. If there is a desensitization of the mouth, as there frequently is in these cases, we often ask the patient to become aware of his lips and tongue as he speaks. Once he has learned to listen and to feel himself speaking, he has made two important steps.

They can also now listen to others, and they have opened the road to the non-verbal in being and communicating. For their compulsive talk drowns out both their environment and their selves. It is their technique of self-interruption. What are they interrupting? Further investigations and experiments help us to find out.

Most often we discover that once we have prevented such patients from using up all their excitement—all their emotional investment—in constant chatter and verbalism, they show tremendous anxiety. Talking has become a compulsion with them, and like all compulsions there is great stress if it is interrupted.

There are, besides the shuttle techniques, still other short-cuts to awareness that we can use. The shuttle technique sharpens awareness by giving the patient a clearer sense of the relationships in his behavior. These other techniques, by encouraging self-expression, also produce both greater awareness and greater self-support.

There are several schools besides ours which make use of the method of self-expression as a means to re-identification. All of them are essentially integrative approaches, but I would like to select Moreno's psychodramatic technique as one of the most lively and as a further demonstration of how we can apply the shuttle technique.

Moreno's way of handling the psychodramatic situation is essentially to ask the patient to switch over from one role to another—for instance, from the harassed child to the nagging mother. That way the patient can realize that his nagging super-ego is his fantasized mother (his introjection), that actually he himself is doing the nagging, that he is not just listening to it but is nagging and being nagged at the same time. Its therapeutic significance is that it facilitates the release of the clinch, the constant quarrel between topdog and underdog, not by adjustment, but by integration.

The psychodramatic technique shows its value in the follow-up to the treatment of the headache we talked about in an earlier chapter. You will remember that ultimately this manifestation boiled down to the patient's statement of two mutually contradictory imperatives: "Don't cry," and "Leave me alone." Now the stage is set for a psychodrama in fantasy. The patient, realizing that the statement demonstrates a split in his own personality, can actually play out both the "don't cry" and the "leave me alone" roles. While he is playing the "don't cry" part, he may discover "I cry when I want to," or "I don't care if I am a sissy," and actually feel his defiance. While he is playing the "don't cry" part, he may feel his contempt for people who behave like sissies. And yet, a minute or two later, he may whisper, sympathetically, "don't cry." At that moment the negative cathexis—people who cry are fools and sissies—changes to a positive one—I feel for people who cry—and the road opens for integration. Perhaps now he will experience his "leave me alone" as "don't interrupt my crying for the wrong reason, for the reason that I'm a sissy. Interrupt it by feeling sorry for me." And the session might finally end up with a need for confluence—"I cry because I have to leave you, but

I don't want you to see it; I don't want to show you how much I need you."

We are now back were we started in the first place. We are back to the patient's lack of self-support. But there is a great difference. The patient is now miserable not, as Freud would say, for neurotic but for human reasons. In our language we would say that now he is no longer concerned with his dissociation, his headache, but with himself. He is, at this moment, fully unified, unhappy in his loneliness. But he expresses it, becomes fully aware of it, and now he may be ready to take the next step, to take responsibility for it and do something about it.

When the patient first came into the consulting room, bearing his headache with him, he was certainly not in *contact* with the therapist. He was in contact with his headache, and his headache was in contact with the therapist. He offered for contact his headache as others offer a mask or a facade. The patient will not part with the mask as long as his feeling of safety behind it outweighs the discomfort of wearing it, and he will certainly object to having his mask torn off his face. The fact that he brought his headache into therapy means that he was ready to acknowledge an unfinished situation; in this respect he was at one with the therapist. It is as if he said: "Make me feel so comfortable that I don't need this symptom or mask or persona or armor." But the therapist could not make him feel comfortable, for the patient was not in contact with him, but with his symptom, the headache.

This is a good example of how we work with psychosomatic symptoms in general. Although the interruption is taking place on the somatic level, where it displays itself in this case as a headache, we have to complete the picture by finding the fantasy that promotes the interruption. We invariably find, when we do this, that the patient will fantasize some command which is opposed to his demand. In this case, the demand was "leave me alone." The commands were "don't cry!" and "a man doesn't cry," and "don't be a sissy!" There might even be a command reinforced by a threat: "If you don't stop crying I'll give you something to cry about!" In other words, the patient behaves as if somebody was ordering him to interrupt his tears. Whatever phrases were impressed on him in the past are now his, and he fantasizes and obeys them.

We can deal with these commands without delving into the unconscious, for there are two possibilities once we have reached this point. Either the patient is aware that he is making inhibiting demands on himself, which is usually the case, or he is not. In the latter case, he will be aware of the demands, but as a projection, as an assumption that the therapist is the one who is opposed to his crying. Once he has gathered enough strength to burst out into "leave me alone," he can take a stand against the counter demand, whether he localizes it as part of his own anti-self (an introjection) or in the therapist as the frustrator of his spontaneous feelings. If he localizes it in the therapist, the next step, (which again has nothing to do with the unconscious) is taken when the patient sees the paradox of accusing the therapist of wanting to interfere with his crying at the same time that he sees the possibility that the therapist might have been in favor of it. If the therapist has taken no sides in this controversy, which is, after all, not his but the patient's, the patient will discover for himself the absurdity of making the therapist responsible for his interruptions, and he will see the symptom as his own responsibility. And so, by the time the session is over, the patient is in *contact with himself*, and this is the first step to making contact with others.

You may have noticed that, in the dissolution of the headache, we made use of some of Reich's findings. I do not want to enter into the violent controversy over Reich or the equally sharp controversy over Hubbard, but I do at this point want to say that I have found their work in certain areas valuable as an adjunct to the awareness technique. Wherever else they may have gone astray, Reich's work on motoric interruptions (the headache, for example) and Hubbard's work with the sensorically experienced return (the cafeteria episode, for example) and with verbal interruptions can provide the therapist with extremely useful tools in the restitution of the functions of the self.

The sensorially experienced return is not new. This method was described more than a decade ago, using the procedure of asking the patient to fill in more and more details of the actually visualized situation. This is re-experiencing on the fantasy level. As far as verbal interruptions are concerned, the idea of repetition has also been used extensively. Repeating over and over the significant maxims of the past, which are actually among the patient's introjections, can also have a therapeutic effect. These maxims apparently have had a profound effect on the patient, as we saw in the headache case. However, I differ from Hubbard in believing that these maxims have their effect not through a traumatic experience but through their every-day intrusion into the patient's life.

There is one disadvantage to any of these techniques: the patient must already be able to express himself to a certain degree. And for the psychodrama he must be able to identify with a role he dislikes. But even if the techniques provide us with no more than an experiment in ferreting out the patient's resistances against self-expression, they are very useful.

Another important therapeutic technique is the approach to the areas of confusion via the manifest interruptions. Confusion is a bad support for contact, and the patient's problem is often displayed in his areas of confusion. Before I discuss how this technique works, however, let me say that the experience of confusion is very, very unpleasant and, like anxiety, shame and disgust, we have a strong desire to annihilate it—by avoidance, by verbalism, or by any other kind of interruption. And yet a good part of the fight against neurosis is won merely by helping the patient to become aware of, to tolerate, and to stay with his confusion and its correlative, blanking out. Although confusion is unpleasant, the only real danger is in interrupting it and consequently becoming confused in action. For confusion, like any other emotion, if left alone to develop uninterrupted, will not remain confusion. It will be transformed into a feeling which is experienced more positively and which can produce appropriate action.

Confusion is generally associated with a lack of

understanding accompanied by a need to understand. The only real guarantee of total freedom from confusion is complete unconcern with understanding. If I am among a group of people who are talking about higher mathematics and I feel a lack of interest it is possible to withdraw: "This is none of my business." But if, for one reason or another, I become interested, my limited knowledge of the subject is bound to make me confused. Confusion, in other words, usually results from an effort to make contact in an area in which, for one reason or another, contact is not possible—perhaps there is not enough understanding to support good contact, perhaps there is not enough interest but there is a need to show interest. Most people try to handle their confusions, because they are so unpleasant, by interrupting them with speculations, interpretations, explanations, and rationalizations. This is the pattern of many neurotics, and especially intellectuals. And it is almost encouraged by certain forms of therapy. Much of Freudian analysis, for example, is based on the error that symbolic, intellectual knowledge is equal to understanding. But such knowledge is usually itself an interruption, a premature arresting of development, leaving behind itself a trail of existential confusion. This in turn contributes to a lack of self-support, to the need for external support, and to the development of a narrow orientation, which has to come from the environment and not from the individual.

Although considerable attention has been paid to the factor of confusion in dealing with psychosis, little attention has been paid to its role in neurosis. Yet every patient in therapy is himself a picture of confusion. And this the therapist cannot fail to see if he will just observe what is going on right under his nose. Every "er" and "ah," every breaking up of a sentence, covers a small or large area of confusion. Each one is an attempt to hang on and maintain *contact,* while the patient's real need is to *withdraw.*

Once the patient has learned to accept the fact that he has areas of confusion, he will be willing to cooperate with the therapist. If he returns to the gaps in his speech he can recover much material which he blanked out or brushed aside during his interruption. Although this material will often be irrelevant, it provides all sorts of helpful clues as to what the patient is doing on the fantasy level. For during these times of confusion he is engaging in faded motoric behavior (all hiding under the collective name of thinking) and much of the activity which is missing in his day-to-day behavior and which constitutes some of the unfinished business of his neurosis, can be found tucked away in those crevices, right here and now.

Let me present a few examples of how this works in practice. The blank, as I said before, is the correlative of confusion. It is an interruption of confusion, the effort to wipe it out completely. This we see most often in dealing with the problem of visualization and visual imagination, areas of blind or nearly blind spots for many patients.

If we ask a patient to visualize something, he may tell us that his fantasy images are hazy. When we ask him to go on, he might continue and report that it is as if they are in a cloud or a fog. This fog or cloud the therapist considers to be a self-concept, a character structure, a system of verbalizations. Apparently the patient has to put a smoke screen around his images and shroud them in a cloud. And the therapist should not be deceived by the patient's complaint that he would like to be able to visualize clearly. Although this is doubtless true, it is not the whole story. We can assume that he must have at least some areas where he has to prevent himself from looking, otherwise he would not go to the trouble of making himself half fantasy blind. If the patient can stay with his fog long enough, it will clear up.

Take the case where the fog cleared into a whitish grey, which the patient reported was like a stone wall. The therapist asked the patient if he could fantasize climbing over that wall. And when the patient did, it developed that there were green pastures there. The wall had enclosed the patient's jail; he was a prisoner.

Our patient may have, on the other hand, a complete blank. He sees black. Suppose he describes the blackness as a black velvet curtain. Now we have our patient and a prop. We can ask him in fantasy to open the curtain. And often enough he will discover behind it that which he was hiding from himself. Perhaps his blackness is literally nothing, a blindness. We can still get some orientation by asking him to play the blind man.

The final step in dealing with the areas of confusion is an eerie experience, often approaching a miracle when it first occurs. Eventually, of course, it becomes routine and is taken for granted. We call it *withdrawal into the fertile void.*

To be able to withdraw into the fertile void two conditions must be obtained. One must be able to stay with one's techniques of interrupting it. Then one can enter the fertile void, which is a state something like a trance, but unlike the trance is accompanied by full awareness. Many people have the experience before falling asleep, and the phenomenon has been described as hypnogogic hallucination.

The person who is capable of staying with the experience of the fertile void—experiencing his confusion to the utmost—and who can become aware of everything calling for his attention (hallucinations, broken up sentences, vague feelings, strange feelings, peculiar sensations) is in for a big surprise. He will probably have a sudden "aha" experience; suddenly a solution will come forward, an insight that has not been there before, a blinding flash of realization or understanding.

What happens in the fertile void is a schizophrenic experience in miniature. This, of course, few people can tolerate. But those who find confidence, having successfully cleared away a few areas of confusion, and having found that they did not fall to pieces completely in the process, will acquire the courage to go into their junkyards and return more sane than when they went in. The most difficult part of the whole experiment is to abstain from an intellectualizing and verbalizing of the on-going process. For this would be an interruption and would put the experimenter in the position of being split between the explaining onlooker and the experiencing performer. The experience of the fertile void is neither objective nor subjective. Nor is it introspection.

It simply is. It is awareness without speculation about the things of which one is aware.

The extremes of the reaction to the idea of the fertile void can be typified in the intellectualizer on the one hand and the artist on the other. The former might say: "Have you suddenly gone mad? This is utter nonsense." But the latter would probably greet the idea thusly: "What's all the excitement about? I spend most of my time in this state. If I'm working and I get stuck, I just relax or doze off and the block goes."

The aim of consulting the fertile void is basically to deconfuse. In the fertile void, confusion is transformed into clarity, emergency into continuity, interpreting into experiencing. The fertile void increases self-support by making it apparent to the experimenter that he has much more available than he believed he had.

Let us return for a moment to the approach to the areas of confusion through the interruptions in which they manifest themselves. Even in this work we can operate successfully only within an extremely limited space of time.[1] Three minutes is often all the area we can cover and recover in toto if we use a mental microscope. It is all very well for the Freudians to demand a recovery of the total life span as a goal for psychoanalysis, but try to experiment for yourself and see if you can recover exactly what you or someone else said or did only a few minutes ago. There are, of course, some people who can do this. They are the type whom Jaensch called eidetic persons. Goethe was such a one. These people register with photographic fidelity on a presomantic level. They register everything they sense, meaningful or not, and they can consequently make use of all their recordings when they want to.

As for the rest of us, and we are the majority, we can restore quite a bit of the lost eidetical faculty through the fertile void and other means of eliminating the interruptions and blanks. One only has to consider that every one of us has developed his own style, his own character. Our patients' interruptions and dissociations will show up in their Rohrschach tests, their

---

[1]This insight is the contribution of my colleage, Dr. Paul Weiss.

handwriting, and their behavior. They will manifest themselves in the smallest details of thinking and feeling. If we change the patient's attitude about the interrupting behavior he presents in the consulting room, his changed attitude will eventually spread and finally engulf his style, his character, his mode of life. His behavior here and now is a microscopic cross section of his total behavior. If he sees how he structures his behavior in therapy, he will see how he structures it in every-day life.

7 | WHO IS LISTENING?

When the patient walks into the consulting room, for the first time or the twentieth, he brings with him all the unfinished business of the past. Yet out of this multitude of possible events, he brings one event at a time into the foreground. Muddy as his gestalt formations are, even they have form and organization; if they were utterly fragmented he could not operate at all. What the patient brings into the foreground is always dictated by the ruling survival impulse operating at the time. Although the connection is often remote, it is our job in therapy to trace it through. Usually we find that this dominant need is for security or approval from the therapist. We have expounded in detail the specific bias of our school: that the patient comes for help and for him help means environmental support, since he is lacking in self-support.

This above explanation seems to come closer to hitting the mark than does any other. Yet we cannot in any specific case know it to be true unless the patient states it to us convincingly. Since the goal of therapy must be related to the patient's experience of his needs, and since he may not experience his needs in this fashion, perhaps we should talk in terms of an even more general goal, and one on which all schools of psychotherapy agree: successful therapy frees in the patient the ability to abstract and to integrate his abstractions.

To do this, the patient must come to his "senses." He must learn to see what is there, and not what he imagines to be there. He must stop hallucinating, transferring, and projecting. He must stop retroflecting and interrupting himself. He must liberate his semantic faculties. He must understand himself and others, and stop twisting and distorting meanings through the off-axis glasses of introjection, prejudices, and convictions. Then he will acquire freedom of action (which is part of health) by transcending the limits of his specific character, and by learning to cope with each new situation as a new situation, and to cope with it by making use of his total potential.

Since the therapist's abstractions are dictated by his own interruptions and by the things he looks for in the patient, how can he set out to help? Ideally, the therapist would act in compliance with the demands of the Eastern sages: "make yourself empty so that you can be filled," or with Freud's rephrasing of that concept in the demand that the therapist's attention be free-floating and he himself free from complexes.

But such an ideal therapist does not exist—and I am not sure he would be any help if he did. For he would be a registering and computing machine; not a human being. He would be free from private and personal troubles, preferences, and limitations. In short, he would be free from himself. If he were genuinely bothered by a toothache, for instance, he would be expected to bracket off his pain and free his attention entirely for the patient.

The real-life, flesh and blood therapist will inevitably display his own personality and his own prejudices in the therapeutic situation. The associationist will look for associations; that is, verbal and pictorial content. The behaviorist will look for verbal and motoric operations. The moralist will look for good and bad attitudes. The Gestaltist will look for finished and unfinished situations.

But the more the therapist relies on his convictions and prejudices, the more he has to depend on speculation to figure out what is going on within the patient. Though many of these psychiatric speculations have been so generally accepted that they have assumed almost the character of reflexes—the phallic symbol hidden in every elongated body, for instance—does not alter the fact that they are speculations and fixed abstractions, like the neurotic's fixed abstractions. As such, they prevent the therapist from seeing anything else.

In other words, whatever we say about the patient's interruptions, fixed abstractions, etc., applies in a lesser degree to the therapist. There is neither a clear-cut qualitative difference between the two, nor is there an absolute equality. There is a hierarchy of greater or lesser freedom from neurosis. In our group therapy sessions, we often find two patients playing a folie à deux, and invariably it develops that the one with less need for environmental support (in other words, the less neurotic one) will be the therapist—that is, he will facilitate the other's development—even if that other is more intent on playing the therapist.

If the therapist has a strong power drive, he will not assist the patient towards self-assertion, but on the contrary will prevent him from even reaching towards it. If he needs the support of rigid theories to make up for his lack of self-support, he will squash the patient by ascribing any difference in point of view to resistance. If the therapist is deeply withdrawn, he will talk about interpersonal relationships, but he will not reach the patient.

In all these cases, and in the many others which are possibilities, he will actually be falling for the patient's manipulations, for he will be unaware that the patient's superficial acceptance of his preachings and interpretations will produce no changes in behavior.

Usually there are three courses open to the therapist, regardless of his bias or theoretical approach. One is sympathy, or involvement in the total field—awareness of both the self and the patient. Another is empathy—a kind of identification with the patient which excludes the therapist himself from the field and thus excludes half the field. In empathy, the therapist's interest is centered exclusively around the patient and his reactions. The ideal therapist I mentioned earlier is an empathist. Lastly, there is apathy—disinterest, represented by the old psychiatric joke, "who listens?" Obviously, apathy gets us nowhere.

Most psychiatric schools, in their quest for an ideal

therapist, look for him to be empathetic. This develops partly out of their pre-field, dualistic approach. But even so, there is a good reason for the reduction of sympathy to empathy. If the therapist is in sympathy with his patient, he may be inclined to give the latter all the environmental support he wants, or to become defensive and feel guilty if he does not. Therapists often have experiences in which they become too involved with their patients; they do not realize the tremendously subtle nature of the patient's manipulatory techniques. In these cases, therapy can be unsuccessful. For to bring about the transformation from external to self-support, the therapist must frustrate the patient's endeavors to get environmental support. This he cannot do if sympathy blinds him to their manipulations.

Yet if the therapist withholds himself, in empathy, he deprives the field of its main instrument, his intuition and sensitivity to the patient's on-going processes. He must, then, learn to work with sympathy and at the same time with frustration. These two elements may appear to be incompatible, but the therapist's art is to fuse them into an effective tool. He must be cruel in order to be kind. He must have a relational awareness of the total situation, he must have contact with the total field—both his own needs and his reactions to the patient's manipulations and the patient's needs and reactions to the therapist. And he must feel free to express them.

Actually, if you examine this proposal for a moment, you will see that it comes closer than any other approach to making the consulting room a microcosm of life. In our daily relations with people—if they are not clouded over by hostility and other unfinished businesses—this is the situation that is obtained. A truly satisfactory and healthy relationship between any two people demands of each of them the ability to blend sympathy with frustration. The healthy person does not trample on the needs of others, nor does he permit his own needs to be trampled on. Neither is he resentful of his partner's assertion of his own rights.

Of course, the other therapeutic procedure of empathy is also like a real-life situation. But the weakness is that it is like precisely those situations which engender and strengthen neurotic development. There can be no true contact in empathy. At its worst it becomes confluence. What about the therapist whose approach is consistently a frustrating one? He is duplicating the situations of constant interruption which the patient has incorporated into his own life and which show themselves as neurosis.

With sympathy alone, the therapist becomes the patient; if we were to talk in old-fashioned terms, we could say he spoils the patient. With frustration only, the therapist becomes the hostile environment, with which the patient can cope only in a neurotic way. In either case, therapy gives the patient no incentive to change.

In sympathy, as in all forms of confluence, the contact boundary is absent. The therapist becomes so much the patient that he can have absolutely no perspective on the latter's problems. He is immersed in the field so completely that he cannot be witness to it. I have known therapists who had such strong needs to mother and to be helpful that they were in chronic confluence with their patients. It is hardly surprising that they should have been very much liked. Their patients depended on them completely, and so no decisive change could occur. If there is too much identification, the therapist can frustrate the patient only as little as he can frustrate himself. And that is nil in those areas of confusion and crisis which are relevant for the production of neurosis.

There is one exception. The empathetic, non-frustrating technique is helpful in the initial phase of treatment of psychosis. Some therapists, notably Fromm-Reichmann, Rosen and Steinfeld, use precisely this approach. Their intuitions of the patient's wants, and their ability to make contact is high. And in the case of psychosis, frustration is already present in the patient to such a high degree that the therapist does not need to produce any. His contact with the patient can itself facilitate the transformation of support. But first the patient must become aware of, and, if possible, develop enough self-support from communication alone to enable him to express his needs, even though he may speak in a language which is incomprehensible to most of us. In dealing with psychotics, we are very careful not to use the tool of frustration too much. We are careful, too, to let them and their behavior—rather than our fantasies and theories about psychosis—guide us.

A demonstration of Gestalt therapy was made in a large mental institution with a patient who had been, for several years, in a close to catatonic state. No one and nothing had been able to reach her. When she communicated at all, she said only that she felt nothing. I noticed, when I began to work with her, that there was a slight trace of moisture in her eyes. Since this might have been indicative of a desire to cry, I asked the patient if she would be willing to repeat, several times, the phrase "I won't cry." (This repetition technique has already been mentioned.) The patient was quite compliant. She droned out the phrase several times—tonelessly, expressionlessly, dully. I noticed, however, that while she was mechanically repeating the phrase, she was slapping her arm against her hip. And so I asked her what that movement reminded her of. Then she burst into speech.

"It's like a mother hitting a child . . . all my mother can do is pray for me."

"Can you pray for yourself?" I asked her.

More animated than at the beginning of the session, but still rather apathetic, she began repeating some prayers. This went on for a while. The prayers were now sensible, now pure mumbo-jumbo. But all of a sudden she called out, pleadingly, "God give me health!" And she broke into a torrent of tears.

This was the first time she had shown any emotion at all. But even more significant, her prayer was a form of self-expression. It was, for the first time, a statement of her needs. It was the opening to her self. And just as the neurotic transforms a repression or a resistance into an expression he is demonstrating some degree of self-support—so this psychotic began to discover, in her outburst, that she had at least enough support available within her to make her needs known.

The completely frustrating approach and the sadistic attitude are actually the stock in trade of those therapists who, in dread of a counter-transference and fearful of their own feelings, present the patient with a poker-face. They would deny it vociferously, but they frustrate the patient through their apathy.

Can we call them sadists? Sadism itself can be defined as unnecessary cruelty. But this definition sounds like a loose formulation. Is not all cruelty unnecessary? Apparently not. Animals kill one another and we ourselves kill steers and pigs for meat. True, the cut-and-can-fed urbanite lives quite removed from the primitive cruelties of life, but he replaces the horrors of the slaughterhouse and the jungle with his horror movies and Mickey Spillanes. Hurting as a fixed pattern of making contact is sadism, but hurting as a means or meaning can be beneficial. We hurt our children when we deny them unreasonable requests, but this is not sadism. We are cruel in order to be kind; this is essentially the meaning of such maxims as "spare the rod and spoil the child," although in application it is not always easy to say how much of this may be a rationalization to cover up the sensual satisfaction of beating, which without question would be sadism.

It seems unnecessary frustration, and therefore sadism, to impose unnecessary suffering on the patient in therapy. Too many therapists present their patients with long lists of "thou shalt nots." They force taboos of abstention on them, they blame them for their resistances. If the therapist has a strong power drive, his reasons for making these demands are sadistic. But usually this is not the case. Usually the therapist believes, in good faith, that by limiting the patient's behavior outside the consulting room, he reduces the frustrations the patient will suffer. Here he makes a mistake. These frustrations are out of control anyway; if they were not, the patient would not be in therapy. And we do not change environmental support into self-support by increasing our patient's frustrations in daily life. What we frustrate is his endeavor to control us by his neurotic manipulations. This forces him to fall back on his own resources and develop self-support. Then he can direct all his manipulatory skill towards the satisfaction of his real needs.

The over-frustrated patient will suffer, but he will not develop. And he will find, with the neurotic's shrewd intuition and distorted vision, all kinds of ways to circumvent the long-range frustrations the therapist imposes on him.

But frustration must be used. I had a patient who had only three months available for therapy; at the end of that period he was to leave the city. Whether in this case it was the spadework of other therapists, or the pressure of time, or my own skill and the techniques of Gestalt therapy that produced important improvements in him I am not prepared to say. But improvements undeniably occurred. And they were so apparent that the patient left feeling that I was a miracle-worker.

When he first appeared, he was nearly mute. He felt weak and incapable; he felt that he had to run away from people—he could not carry on any conversation at all and he suffered real torments if he had to be in any kind of social situation. Additionally, he had a pretty fully developed system of projections; he felt persecuted and was convinced that others thought him a homosexual.

The first six weeks of therapy—more than half the available time—were spent in frustrating him in his desperate attempts to manipulate me into telling him what to do. He was by turn plaintive, aggressive, mute, despairing. He tried every trick in the book. He threw the time barrier up to me over and over again, trying to make me responsible for his lack of progress. If I had yielded to his demands, undoubtedly he would have sabotaged my efforts, exasperated me, and remained exactly where he was.

One day he came in complaining that he behaved like a baby. I then suggested to him that he play the baby, fantasizing all the satisfactions he could get out of that. From that point on, his progress was enormous. He played out, with enormous satisfaction, all of the phases of his development, from infancy through adolescence. He relived and expressed in fantasy any number of disturbing events and unfinished situations. By the time the three months were over, he had reached a point where, having achieved satisfaction in the areas where he had been previously frustrated and blocked, he was able to move on to new satisfactions and self-support.

What I want to demonstrate here is that no development can take place before the patient achieves satisfaction in all areas in which he is confused, blank, or stuck. And the prerequisite for full satisfaction is the patient's sense of identification with all the actions he participates in, including his self-interruptions. A situation can only be finished—which means full satisfaction can only be achieved—if the patient is totally involved in it. Since his neurotic manipulations are ways of avoiding total involvement, they must be frustrated.

For this reason, the analytic and cathartic procedure is as insufficient as is the procedure based on the therapist's attempt at interpretative integration. In the first case, with purely cathartic discharge, there is no transformation of emotion into action, into self-expression and integration. On the contrary, the energy that will support the contact functions is drained off, and the balance of power is in favor of the self-concept. In the second case, although looking upon his behavior as meaningful allays much of the patient's confusion, subtractive therapy—taking away symptoms and confusion—does not develop the self-support we need to make and realize our existential choices. The patient may "understand" himself completely, but he is incapable of doing anything himself.

Gestalt therapy makes the basic assumption that the patient is lacking in self-support, and that the therapist symbolizes the patient's incomplete self. The first step in therapy then is to find out what the patient needs. If he is not psychotic (and even sometimes if he is, as the case described earlier indicated) the patient is partly aware of his needs and can at least partially express them. But there are some areas in which the patient is either unaware of his specific needs, or is blocked in demanding what he wants. Often the therapist finds that the patient is ashamed to make certain requests, equally often he finds that the patient is convinced that the only valuable help he can get is help that is guessed and given without being asked for. Often he does not know how to ask, or he is confused about what he really wants. But once he can express his demands, his orders, his commands, and his requests directly and actually mean what he says, he has made the most important step in all of his therapy. Instead of covering himself over with his techniques of neurotic manipulation, he shows and commits himself to his needs. The self and the supplementing other (the therapist) are now clearly defined and the patient comes face to face with his problem.

The imperative is the primary form of communication. It ranges from the primitive signal to the most elaborately woven network of highly abstract objective statements which render the signals, per se, unrecognizable. Yet we react even to these as if they were signals pure and simple, imperatives, and demands. There was a time not too long ago when Einstein's formulations, which we now take for granted, were felt by many scientists to be a challenge. It was to them as if Einstein had said, "Look what I have found. I dare you to accept it or knock it down."

For the neurotic it makes all the difference in the world whether he deals with the therapist through implicit insinuations or through open, explicit demands. In the first case, he is trying to manipulate us to support his neurosis, and we cannot fall for that trick. In the second case, when the patient makes an explicit demand, he has already begun to clarify and discover his lack of being. We must not supply the supplements he is looking for, but now that he begins to recognize his needs he will begin to learn how to satisfy them for himself.

Here, however, we have to distinguish between expressive and impressive speech, that is, between speech which is meant to give vent to one's feelings and demands, and speech which is meant to produce a reaction in someone else. And such instances of relatively pure expression and impression do exist as extremes of the communication scale. To express joy, for example, we do not need anyone around to impress with our state. But to impress, we need an audience and need it badly. In impressive speech we will do anything to get attention. Even if there is nothing to express, we will conjure something up or rake our memories for suitable conversational tid-bits.

Genuine communication is at neither end of the scale. It functions as a field event; it is of concern and it is real to both sender and receiver. The primary demand—which is a genuine communication—is not differentiated into expression or impression. There is a world of difference between the baby's anguished cry, to which a mother responds automatically, and the attention-seeking howling of the spoiled brat, to which the mother might respond—but with anger, not concern.

What is wrong with getting attention? The "hear ye, hear ye," of the town crier, the "Shma Yisroel" of the pious Jew, the "silence in court," the drowning man crying for help—are they not all seeking full attention?

The difference between these cases and the baby on the one hand, and the exhibitionist and the brat on the other, lies in the difference between genuine expression and the "as if" attitude. The brat conjures up his howling and can replace it at any moment with a tantrum or anything else that will interrupt what his mother is doing. He is manipulating, but he is not communicating his real need, which is not attention but may be escape from his boredom. The baby cries for something for which he has no self-support, as does the drowning man. But the brat cries for something in an area in which he should already be self-supportive.

The genuine imperative corresponds to the natural figure-ground formation; it points directly to the positive and the negative cathexis. Kurt Lewin said that the cathected object has an "Aufforderungs character," that is, it is provocative, it has a character of demand. The positively cathected object demands attention, the negatively cathected one annihilation. To annihilate it, we don't necessarily need to destroy it. If there is someone who infuriates and irritates you, you do not have to shoot him, throw him bodily out of the room, or put adhesive tape over his mouth. You merely demand, "Get out," or "shut up."

The imperative is, by its nature, the most powerful tool of moulding the individual into a socially required shape. From the primitive's taboos and the Ten Commandments, down to mother's dos and don'ts, its importance has never been underestimated. There is nothing wrong with the imperative per se; the trouble begins if, for biological or psychological reasons, the receiver is unwilling or unable to receive the message. This is merely another reformulation of our basic thesis on the genesis of neurosis—neurosis arises if there are present, simultaneously, social and personal imperatives which cannot both be met by the same action.

If the demand and the thing demanded are acceptable, the gestalt is closed. The baby's demand for mother, the request of the unsure for guidance, the responsibility relieving commands given the soldier; they are all a unit, they go together hand in glove. They are gracefully accepted. But if there is a resistance and the imperative is executed nevertheless, we have resentment and neurosis. If, on the other hand, the imperative has assumed the status of natural law, "honor thy father and mother," for instance, and is nevertheless rejected, we have either criminality or we have the neurotic feeling of guilt.

The neurotic's trouble usually begins if, in childhood, the imperative is against his grain but is nevertheless accepted in good faith. Then an area of simple or double confusion is created, and whatever decision is made leads to despair.

The command "don't cry," for example, when there is a genuine experience of grief, is a simple confusion. This confusion is compounded if a semantic confusion is tacked on to it. Orders like "act your age," and "behave yourself," and others that have extensive connotations leave the child utterly mixed up. "What is it to act my age?" "What is behaving myself?" We have found in clinical experience that sticklers for detail were often confronted with such vague demands in their childhood.

It is not exaggerating the situation to say that each time a patient has integrated the dissociated parts of a neurotic event like a symptom, and has managed to put across a fully felt imperative—"leave me alone," for example—he has cleared away one area of confusion. This is something he has wanted to say for years, but his introjecting pattern has forced him to interrupt his expression.

But now the patient's demand is a genuine imperative. It expresses his needs. It is meaningful to him and to the therapist. The therapist can and should do what he can to satisfy such truly felt needs and demands, as the mother does what she can to soothe her fretting baby. We could sum up the therapeutic approach presented here and the therapist's use of the tools of frustration and satisfaction by saying that the therapist must frustrate those of his patient's expressions which reflect his self-concept, his manipulatory techniques, and his neurotic patterns. He must satisfy those of the patient's expressions that are truly expressions of the patient's self. If he is to help the patient to any sort of self-realization, he must, by definition, discourage any satisfaction of the patterns which prevent self-realization (the neurosis) and encourage exhibitions of the essential self the patient is trying to find.

This again indicates the degree to which, as therapy progresses, the therapeutic session becomes more and more like the ideal of daily life. As the patient's experience of himself increases, he becomes more self-supportive and better able to make good contact with others. As he casts aside more and more of his neurotic techniques of manipulation, the therapist needs to frustrate him less and less and is more and more able to help him towards satisfaction. As was said earlier, self-support is very different from self-sufficiency. When the patient is discharged from therapy he will not lose his need for other people. On the contrary, he will for the first time derive real satisfactions from his contact with them.

PART II | EYE WITNESS TO THERAPY

PUBLISHER'S NOTE

Fritz Perls might have begun the introduction to this section with his admonition that "Gestalt therapy is a commitment to boredom." Many of us attending his workshops had grown used to seeing what appeared to be miraculous cures. We were jaded by the succession of people working in the hot seat who were suddenly released from self-imposed torture games. In his later years Fritz grew increasingly tired of this game of Lourdes. In a sense this was a come on.

Fritz knew he now had an audience of serious students. In his proposed book *Eye Witness to Therapy* Fritz wanted to start with verbatim film transcripts of introductory gestalt work. He wanted the student to study these films and the transcripts in detail. He did not see his work as enigmatic or miraculous. He believed once we really understood the gestalt process these isolated miracles would all fall in place. He hoped these films and books would de-mystify the cult of Fritz Perls.

The purpose of this volume is to encourage serious introductory study. Richard Bandler chose excerpts that are largely self-explanatory. In later volumes he will present more advanced gestalt work which will be accompanied by commentary by Karl Humiston, Virginia Satir, and other therapists who have lived and worked with Fritz Perls.

There are some obvious problems in studying the transcripts without the film. Fritz placed great emphasis on voice tone, inflection, and non-verbal communication. The films are essential for these dimensions. Also there is a problem with time distortion. The word "pause" can represent two seconds or two minutes, and we read much faster than we talk. A half-hour session can be read in five minutes. All these factors can add to the illusion that Gestalt therapy is instantaneous and defeat a major purpose of this study.

Robert S. Spitzer, M. D.
Editor-in-Chief
Science and Behavior Books

8 | GESTALT IN ACTION

What is Gestalt?

The idea of Gestalt therapy is to change paper people to real people. I know, it's a big mouthful. And, to make the whole man of our time come to life and to teach him to use his inborn potential to be, let's say, a leader without being a rebel, having a center, instead of living lopsided. All these ideas sound very demanding, but I believe it's now possible that we can do it; that we don't have to lie on the couch for years, decades, and centuries without essential changes. The condition under which this can be achieved is this: Again, I have to jump back and talk about the social milieu in which we find ourselves. In the previous decades, the man of society lived for what is right, and he did his job, never mind whether he really wanted the job, or whether he was suited for it. But the whole society was ruled and regulated by 'shouldism' and by puritanism. You did your thing whether you liked it or not. Now I believe the whole social milieu has changed. Puritanism has changed into hedonism. We begin to live for fun, enjoyment, for being turned on. Anything goes as long as it's nice. Sounds good, too. Sounds superior to moralism. It is, however, a very serious setback. Namely, that we have become *phobic* towards pain and suffering. Let me repeat that word—we have become phobic towards pain and suffering. Anything that is not fun or pleasant is to be avoided. So we run away from any frustration that might be painful and try to short-cut it. And the result is a lack of growth. When I talk about the readiness to encounter unpleasantness, I certainly do not mean an education towards masochism; on the contrary, a masochist is a person who's afraid of pain and trains himself to tolerate it. I'm talking about the suffering that goes along with growing up. I'm talking about facing honestly unpleasant situations. And this is very much linked up with the Gestalt approach. I don't want to talk too much about the phenomenon of Gestalt, however. The main idea of Gestalt is that a gestalt is a whole, a complete, in itself, resting whole. As soon as we cut up a gestalt, we have bits and pieces and not a whole anymore. We come across this thing several times, but just let me say that if you have three pieces of wood, here one piece, here one piece, and here one piece, these three pieces of wood are very inaccurate gestalts. If you put them together like that then you see immediately that there's a triangle, but as soon as you take this apart, the triangle disappears and the gestalt disappears. Now, in the biological gestalt formation, the gestalt has a dynamic which regulates all organic life.

The gestalt wants to be completed. If the gestalt is not completed, we are left with unfinished situations, and these unfinished situations press and press and press and want to be completed. Let's say if you had a fight, you really got angry at that guy, and you want to take revenge. This need for revenge will nag and nag and nag until you have become even with him. So there are thousands of unfinished gestalts. How to get rid of these gestalten is very simple. These gestalts will emerge. They will come to the surface. Always the most important gestalt will emerge first. We don't have to dig a la Freud, into the deepest unconscious. We have to become aware of the obvious. If we understand the obvious, everything is there. Every neurotic is a person who doesn't see the obvious. So what we're trying to do in Gestalt therapy is to understand the word 'now,' the present, the awareness and see what happens in the now. And to understand the now will take you anywhere from four weeks to twenty years.

'Now' is such an interesting, difficult concept because on the one hand, you can only work and achieve something if you work in the now and the present. On the other hand, as soon as you make a moralistic demand out of it, you immediately see it's impossible. If you try to grasp the now, it's already gone. It's such a paradox, to work in the now and still be unable to hold on or even to focus on it.

The second point I have to make in regard to our therapy is the word 'how.' In previous centuries, we asked 'why.' We tried to find causes, reasons, excuses, rationalizations. And we thought if we could change the causes we could change the effect. In our electronic age, we don't ask why anymore, we ask how. We investigate the structure, and when we understand the structure, then we can *change* the structure. And a structure in which we are most interested, is the structure of our lifescript. The structure of our lifescript—often called karma or fate—is mostly taken up with self-torture, futile self-improvement games, achievements, and so on. And then two people meet, and they have some different lifescripts, and then they try to force the other person to your lifescript or you're willing to please the other person and efface your needs and become part of his script—and then there is involvement, confusion, fighting; and people get stuck with each other and the whole lifescript is being messed up, which again, is part of the lifescript.

So what we want to do is to reorganize our lifescript. And the ways and means to do it can be understood to quite an extent. Right now, I am interested in meeting some of you and I have to admit I have a very bad memory for names, and I have to know a person pretty well or have a shock or great joy when I meet this person so that I can recall the names. In order to work I brag about the six components of my work. To work I need my skill, the so-called hot seat; which in this case is very beautiful (Laughter), the empty chair, which has the task of taking up roles which you have disowned, and other people which we need to understand our lifescript. We need something which is absent, and I hope maybe today that we don't need it—that is kleenex, my cigarettes, and ashtray, and then I'm in business. (Laughter) So, I invite anyone who wants to come forth and work with me to take the hot seat.

(Don comes up; he is a bearded man, about forty, and teaches art.)

Fritz: Your name is . . . ?

Don: Don.

Fritz: Don. I have only one request to make to you, to use the word 'now,' if possible, in every sentence.

Don: Like now I feel my heart beating. Now I wonder why I'm sitting here. (Laughter) Why did I wish to fill the void? Now I'm wondering what there is to work with.

Fritz: Yah. Let me interrupt you here and switch back to Freud and his psychoanalysis. Freud said, a person who is free of guilt feelings and anxiety is healthy. My own theory about anxiety and guilt is this. Guilt is nothing but unexpressed resentment. And, anxiety is nothing but the gap between the now and the later. As soon as you leave the secure basis of the now and jump into the future, you experience anxiety, or in this case, stagefright. You get excited, your heart begins to race and so on —all the symptoms of stagefright. The fact that we don't very often notice our chronic anxiety is simply that we fill the gap of the now and later with insurance policies, rigid character formations, daydreams, and so on. If we reduce the later to the now, the anxiety is bound to collapse. So, let's do this now. Close your eyes, and tell us in detail, what do you experience now?

Don: Physically, I feel the warmth of one hand in another. I feel, now I feel, um, tension throughout my body. Especially up here. (Points to his chest.)

Fritz: Fine. Can you enter this tension?

Don: It's as if I'm being stretched this way. (Pulls his arms crosswise across his chest.)

Fritz: Can you do this to me? Stretch me.

Don: (Gets up and pulls at Fritz' shoulders.) It's as if I'm being pulled out this way.

Fritz: More. Do it as much as you need to. Okay. Sit down.

Don: Now it's gone away. (Laughter)

Fritz: If you learn to do unto others what you are doing unto yourself you stop repressing yourself and preventing yourself from what you're going to do. I don't understand your need to stretch me—and here I have to shock you—because here I have to introduce one of the technical terms in Gestalt therapy, which is mind-fucking. The very moment we just play these intellectual games, like they do usually in group therapy—they throw opinions on each other, explanations, people interpret each other—so nothing happens except these intellectual word games. So what do you experience now, Don?

Don: My own mind-fucking. (Laughter) Explaining to myself why I would want to stretch you.

Fritz: Okay, let's introduce the empty chair. Ask Don this question.

Don: Don, why do you want to stretch yourself or another person?

Fritz: Now, change seats. And, this is the decisive phrase—start to write your script between the two opponents.

Don: Well, Don, you're not good enough the way you are so you've got to stretch.

Don: Yeh, that's quite possible. One never knows what one's potentials are unless one does stretch. I agree, I should stretch.

Don: Yes, um, you seem to have got the message, and all you have to do is do something about it.

Don: Yeh, I do try to do something about it, um, sometimes. I'm constantly aware that I'm supposed to do something about it. I don't always do something about it. Once in awhile.

Fritz: Oh! We make now the first acquaintance

with one of the most frequent splits in the human personality. That is the topdog-underdog split. The topdog is known in psychoanalysis as the superego or the conscience. Unfortunately, Freud left out the underdog, and he did not realize that usually the underdog wins in the conflict between topdog and underdog. I give you the frequent characteristics of both. The topdog is righteous, some of the time right, but always righteous. He takes for granted that this topdog that tells him he should stretch him to prove the topdog is correct. The topdog always says you should and the topdog threatens if not, then . . . However, the topdog is pretty straightforward. Now the underdog looks for the different method. The underdog says, yeh, or I promise, or I agree (laughter) or mañana, if I only could. So the underdog is a very good frustrator. And then the topdog, of course, doesn't let him get away with it and it praises the use of the rod and so the self-torture game or self-improvement game, whatever you want to call it, goes on year in and year out, year in and year out and nothing ever happens. Right?

Don: Not quite, but . . . the topdog keeps pushing, and he gets . . .

Fritz: Say this to the topdog.

Don: Yeh, you keep pushing and sometimes I give you something but I often feel it isn't adequate enough for you—doesn't quite meet your demands.

Fritz: So be the topdog and demand. What are your demands? You should . . .

Don: You should get much more organized and you could be far more intelligent about how you go about things than you are right now.

Fritz: Okay. Now, again. You do unto others what you do to yourself. Say the same sentence to these people here. You should get better organized.

Don: (Sigh) Bill, if you want to improve, you should get much better organized and make much better use of your time and energy. Ann, you should get much more organized and be more intelligent about how you go about how you go about things and you'll go a lot further. Gail, you can do the same.

Fritz: How do you feel when you say this to others and not to yourself?

Don: I feel that they could tell me to go to hell.

Fritz: (To group.) Tell him to go to hell. You keep on nagging and nagging and no one tells you to go to hell.

Gail: Go to hell.

Don: Haven't I told you often enough (laughter) that you should work harder?

Gail: As a matter of fact, you have.

Don: Ann, can't you work harder? Can't you organize yourself better?

Ann: I don't want to, thank you, Don Babcock. (Laughter)

Don: How about you, Bill? You could go much further if you organized yourself better. You'd be a wealthy man now. (Laughter) You'd have a fantastically successful business if you organized yourself better and worked harder—with your talent.

Fritz: Okay, how do you feel now?

Don: I feel like a very self-righteous . . . (Laughter)

Fritz: How's your stagefright?

Don: Oh, it's sort of gone away.

Fritz: Yes, but this being self-righteous is part of your lifescript and so you need a lot of people you can be self-righteous with.

Awareness

Now this workshop is somewhat different from the usual workshop, but in both cases, there's, we have two things, or one thing in common. In both cases, we are dealing with a learning process. Learning is mostly misunderstood. My definition of learning is to discover that something is possible. It's not just the taking in of some information. And all I want to do here is to show you that it is possible to discover means and ways whereby you can grow and develop your potential, and iron out difficulties in your life. Now this, of course, can not be done in a short workshop. But, maybe I can plant a few seeds, take a few of the covers that will open up possibilities. Again, let me repeat—*learning is to discover that something is possible*. We are using most of our energies for self-destructive games, for self-preventing games. And as I mentioned already, we do this and prevent ourselves from growing. The very moment something unpleasant, something painful comes up, at that moment we become phobic. We run away. We desensitize ourselves. We use all kinds of means and ways to prevent the growth process.

If you try to be aware of what's going on—then, you see, very soon you leave the secure basis of the now, and become phobic. You start running away into the past and start to associate freely, or you run into the future and start to fantasize the terrible things that will befall you if you stay with what's going on or you do all kinds of things. Suddenly you discover that you've taken up too much of the group's time, and this is the task of the therapist or if you work with somebody else—the task of the partner—to see that he or she stays in the focus of the experience and understands the very moment and uncovers what makes him or her run away. There's a very complicated process of self-deception involved. And as I've said before, a little bit of honesty goes a long way and this is what most of us are afraid of—being honest with ourselves and stopping the idea of self-deception. As T.S. Eliot says, "Most of you are self-deceivers taking infinite pains, but seldom are successful." And Eliot said something else, "You're nothing but a set of obsolete responses." And if you are not in the present, you cannot have a creative life.

Again, we have to go another step further and say that neurotic suffering is suffering in imagination—suffering in fantasy. Somebody calls you a son of a bitch, and you think you are suffering. You feel hurt. But you don't really; you don't feel hurt. There are no bruises, there are no actual injuries there. It is your so-called ego or vanity that is hurt. You can even go a step further and say when you feel hurt you actually feel vindictive, and you want to hurt the other person. So, what I'd like to do in the beginning is to take a few of you and ask you to come on the hot seat and work on the phenomenological basis. This means work on the awareness of the on-going process. If you live in the present, you use whatever is available. If you live in your computer or in your thinking machine, or in these obsolete responses or in your rigid way of coping with life, you stay stuck. So let's take a few of you, whoever wants to come forth. And the more stagefright, the better. (Pause. Marek comes and sits in the hot seat.)

Fritz: Let's work very primitively, even if we structure the whole thing a little bit. Rigidly, pompously, for the first moment, you will very soon see the meaning of it. So start with the sentence, 'now I am aware of.'

Marek: Now I am aware of, um, tension in my right arm, now I am aware of faces (smiles) looking in my direction. Now I am aware of you, Fritz. Now I am still aware of my hand. And now I am aware of changing my position to a more relaxed position. Now I am aware of the box in front of me. Now I am aware of waiting for the pressure to be taken off me. (Smiles)

Fritz: You see, at this moment he jumped into the future. The word waiting for means he stopped being aware of what's going on. Except we now reduce his anticipation to the ongoing process—and we do it with the request of 'how.' How covers all possible means of behavior. How do you experience waiting?

Marek: I experience waiting as this moment has tremendous tension here. Definitely tension throughout my whole body, plus a certain fearful blankness is starting to cover my thinking process.

Fritz: Now I have to add what I'm aware of. I'm aware that you're doing a lot of smiling. And even when you talk about unpleasantness—like unpleasant tension—you are still smiling, and to me this is inconsistent.

Marek: (Laughs) This may be true, uh, it's a weapon, I suppose.

Fritz: What are you doing now?

Marek: Intellectualizing?

Fritz: Yes, you're defending yourself. Are you aware of that?

Marek: Yes, now.

Fritz: So, maybe my remark was unpleasant to you?

Marek: Perhaps, a little bit, yes. (Bites lip, smiles)

Fritz: Are you now aware of your smile?

Marek: Uh, don't you like me smiling?

Fritz: Were you aware of what you did with that sentence?

Marek: I thought I expressed a certain amount of hostility, perhaps.

Fritz: You attacked me.

Marek: I didn't mean to attack you, but . . .

Fritz: Now again, are you aware that you're getting defensive?

Marek: Yes. I have a very defensive nature, I think.

Fritz: Okay, now the next one. I just want a short example to reinforce the awareness basis. You see, what we're doing is simply sampling; simply getting acquainted with the on-going process of awareness and how the different people avoid the full involvement in what is there. We can now take the next step and see what you *are* in touch with. There are three possibilities—you can be in touch with the world, you can be in touch with yourself, or you can be in touch with your fantasy life. The fantasy life—or the middle zone—was first discovered by Freud under the name of complex, and it's the middle zone which is the insane part of ourselves. It's the fantasy whenever this fantasy is taken for a real thing.

The real insane person is known as the person who says I am Napoleon, and that he actually believes he is Napoleon. If I say I would like to be Napoleon, you wouldn't call me crazy. If I say, I'm Napoleon, go, march to Austerlitz or whatever it is, you say, what is this queer behavior of that guy? And especially there is a zone in which we are fully and absolutely crazy. That is in our dreams. You see later on, just these dreams, the middle zone, has assumed so much importance in our lives that we are out of touch with the reality which is either that reality of the world, or the other reality of our authentic self. All right, (turns to Don in the hot seat) will you start with this experiment—now I am aware of.

Don: Um, I'm immediately aware um that your attention has turned from me, uh, turned on to me, that my voice seems quavering. Um, that my mind is sort of split between a fantasy and being aware of my body.

Fritz: Now, my mind is split between fantasy and body. For me, mind *is* fantasy. (Pause) And when you say my mind is split, I guess you say my attention is split.

Don: Right. Exactly. If my body is in my mind, my mind is on my body, that's where my attention is. Uh, I still feel a quivering, like a shivering leaf in my chest. I notice that my hand is fluttering around a little bit. I point it to my chest. Uh, the quivering is rising into my throat. I'm aware that I'm staring at the carpet. People's feet are moving.

Fritz: Are you also aware that you're avoiding looking at me, looking at anybody?

Don: Yeah. I'm not looking—before now—people seem very tense, sort of suspended. But very real.

Fritz: So, now you can start shuttling between self-awareness and world awareness. The self-awareness is symbolized by the word 'I' and the world by the word 'you.' I and thou. And if you have too much I, you are self-centered, withdrawn and so on. If you have too much thou, you're paranoic or aggressive or a businessman or something like that.

Don: (To group) Well, I have been looking at you. I am looking at you now and the more I look at you the less quivering I feel inside myself. Uh, some of you seem to look right straight at me, and some of you look out from the side of your head or from the top of your head. Shirley, you seem to be looking at me from below/above. Dawn, you seem to be from the side of your head, and other people . . .

Fritz: Now, shuttle back to self-awareness.

Don: (Cough) Uh, I feel a great ball of tension in here. My mouth is dry.

Fritz: Now shuttle back to world-awareness.

Don: Uh, I seem to want to focus on one or . . .

Fritz: You're still in the 'I.'

Don: Um, Gordon, you're looking very confident, but a bit fierce. (Smiles)

Fritz: Now you saw him. Now shuttle back to yourself.

Don: That makes me feel confident that you're (chuckles) confident.

Fritz: Now you see you get an integration. World and I are one. If I *see,* I don't see, the world just is there. And as soon as I see, I strain, I pierce, and do all kinds of things except having a world. Okay, thank you. (Pause, Penny comes to the hot seat.)

Fritz: Your name is?

Penny: Penny.

Fritz: Penny, yah, you're Penny.

Penny: Um, I'm aware of my heart beating. My hands are cold. I'm afraid to look out and my heart's still pounding.

Fritz: Were you aware how you avoided me? You

looked at me and quickly looked away. What are you avoiding? Were you aware of smiling when you looked at me?

Penny: Mmmmhhhmmm.

Fritz: What kind of smile did you experience when you looked at me?

Penny: I'm afraid. I try to hide my fear. (Holds back tears, bites lip)

Fritz: Is your fear pleasant or unpleasant? Do you feel comfortable with your fear?

Penny: Yes. My heart's not pounding so much, anymore.

Fritz: Mmmhhmm. Now, try to get more of the rhythm of contact and withdrawal. Of coping and withdrawal. This is the rhythm of life. You flow towards the world and you withdraw into yourself. That is the basic rhythm of life. In winter we are more withdrawn—in summer more outgoing. During the night, we withdraw deeply and during the day we are more busy with coping. If I miss a word, I withdraw to my dictionary, and come back when I've found the word to fill in the gap in the sentence. So this rhythm goes on and on, I and thou, together form a unit. And if you have this middle zone, then this middle zone comes between you and the world and stops you from functioning adequately. In this middle zone especially, there are catastrophic expectations, or complexes that distort your view of the world and so on. We have to deal with this later. Right now, I want to give you a feel of the contact and withdrawal situation. Withdraw as deep as possible. Go even away from this room, and then come back and see us again. And see what will happen if you try this rhythm.

Penny: Coming back is more comfortable.

Fritz: So go on with this rhythm. Again, close your eyes. Withdraw, and each time verbalize where you are going to. Are you going to the beach? Are you going into your thinking bit?

Are you going into some muscular tensions? Then come out again, and say what you are aware of.

Penny: I feel more relaxed. It's, it seems more, uh, just go inside myself. (Pause) But, I don't want to stay. (Pause) I get bored with it.

Fritz: You remember what our basic contract was? Always to say, now I am aware. So, when you looked at me what were you aware of?

Penny: (Pause) Groping for an answer.

Fritz: Yah. You see, apparently this is now unpleasant. So, you stop being aware. You start to think and play around with probing, looking. In other words you are still withdrawn into your computer. You're not with me. You're not in the world yet. So, close your eyes. Go away. (Sigh from Penny) Last time you went away, you found boredom. Is your feeling of boredom pleasant or unpleasant?

Penny: Unpleasant.

Fritz: Ah, so stay with it and tell us what is unpleasant about being bored.

Penny: (Pause) I feel frustrated. I want to do something.

Fritz: Say this again.

Penny: I want to do something. (Pause, closes her eyes)

Fritz: Now, come back. What do you experience, here, now?

Penny: (Looks around) The colors are bright.

Fritz: Pardon?

Penny: The colors are bright.

Fritz: The colors are bright. That is a good symptom. This is what we call in Gestalt therapy, a mini-satori. She begins to wake up. Did you notice—the world becomes real, the colors are bright. This sounded very genuine and spontaneous. (Pause) Will you come forward? Your name is?

Ann: Ann.

Fritz: Ann. (Pause)

Ann: I'm aware of a tension in my head. It's all around my head. I feel it as a tingling and a tightening. Uh, like my head is going to sleep, like a limb goes to sleep. And it, uh, burns, as well.

Fritz: Now, go to the world. What are you aware of in your environment?

Ann: (Pause, she looks around and starts to cry) I'm aware of, a boy here looking very kindly towards me, you. I feel him very kind and understanding.

Fritz: Now we come to another condition in Gestalt therapy. We always try to establish contact. Can you say the same sentence to him instead of gossiping about him? Say this to him.

Ann: I feel, I feel, that you're, that you feel very kindly and sympathetic.

Fritz: Now withdraw again. (Pause) Were you aware that you were crying a little bit?

Ann: Mmmhhmm.

Fritz: So why don't you say so?

Ann: I'm aware, I'm aware of crying. Um, sort of just being upset. (Sighs) I feel that it's sort of, uh, the upsetness is sort of, um, patterns sort of broken up in some way.

Fritz: Now come back to us. This time, you came to me; how do you experience me?

Ann: I experience you as, uh, a very, very, uh, sort of real, sort of definite person, who's quite close and is, uh, is here with me. Well, not with me, but with everybody that's here.

Fritz: Now go away from me again. Parting is such sweet sorrow. (Grins)

Ann: (Pause) I feel, I'm aware of, uh, tension in my head. Sort of a tightening particularly above my ears.

Fritz: Can you close your eyes?

Ann: Mmmhhmm.

Fritz: And find out how you do this. What are you tensing, how do you produce your tightness?

Ann: (Pause) I feel I pull things in and I pull things together.

Fritz: Mmmhhmm. So come back once more.

Ann: (Looks around) I feel the, uh, group, uh, is sort of opened up a bit.

Fritz: Yah. Good. Thank you. (Shakes her hand) Now, this is the basis of expanding awareness. We don't need LSD or any of the artificial means of jazzing us up. If we produce our own awareness, if we do it ourselves and not rely on artifacts, we have all the basis for growth that we need. So, let's have a break.

Marriage

We spoke yesterday about the lifescript of a person, and this lifescript has a number of other people involved, in that we need other people for a certain amount of support for our self-esteem. We need other people for feeding or sexual needs. But in many cases our lifescript demands marriage. And the trouble in a marriage starts if the spouse does not fit into that lifescript. In other words, if that person is not in love with that spouse, but with an image of what the spouse should be. Now very rarely does the image of the spouse and the real person fit. So there are frustrations and difficulties, especially if a person is cursed with perfectionism. Then, you're really in for trouble. The curse of perfectionism is the worst thing that can befall any person. Once you're a perfectionist, you have a yardstick, where you can always beat yourself and beat other people, because you demand the impossible. And once you start demanding the impossible from your partner, then the resentment starts—the blaming game, the irritations, and so on and so on.

So, in our marriage game, we can't do much more than just playing games here and finding some basis for where people stand with each other. Let's start with the same kind of communication approach that we used in the awareness. In other words, I and you. Let's first get you two here (Don and Claire sit in the hot seats) and you will face the enemy. (Laughter) So, your name is?

Claire: Claire.

Don: Don.

Fritz: Claire, Don and I would like you to do this in exchange—withdrawing into yourself with the word 'I' and then come back to Don and say 'you.' Go back again—I and you. And you do the same . . . shuttle and see to what degree a simple communication is possible. What we are most interested in, of course, is what kind of communication you avoid. Of course, there are plenty of catastrophic expectations. If I tell you what I really think about you, you will not like me, you will leave me, or whatever the catastrophic expectations are.

Claire: Uh, I find it hard to go into myself. (Pause) I want to go out to you, and uh, assure you that I'm with you.

Fritz: Go back again.

Claire: Go into myself, and I want to be myself too. (Smiles)

Fritz: Are you aware that you are full of good intentions—I want, I want, I want this. You're not telling us what you're aware of, but what you want. In other words, you're not in the now, you're not telling us what you're doing but what you want. Okay, Don.

Don: Um, I'm back to the clutch in myself, here, and I find it's easy to go into myself, and uh, more difficult to come to you. And, uh, I think, I, I was, was aware, am now remembering when I looked at all the people, I didn't look at you when I sat here, before.

Fritz: This is very simple. A clear symptom of avoidance. If you avoid looking at another person, it means that you're not open. Your turn, Claire.

Claire: (Pause) I'm aware of tension, inside myself. Sort of a throbbing. (Pause) Quivering sort of expectation. I'm aware of your calm. (Smiles) Uh, your certainty, what's underneath. I'm aware of my inadequacy to express myself. Holding my thumb. Being unsure.

Fritz: Are you aware of your voice?

Claire: Quiet.

Fritz: Can you talk to Don about your voice and what you're doing to him with your voice?

Claire: Well, I hope it's not so quiet that you have to, to strain to hear me.

Fritz: Your hoping. What are you doing?

Claire: I'm talking softly. Hesitantly. (Pause) Uncertainly.

Fritz: By the way, this low voice is always a symptom of hidden cruelty. It's one of the best means of torturing other people.

Claire: It's not always soft. (Smiles)

Fritz: Don.

Don: I'm aware that I'm calmer now. And uh, I think I'm calm partly because I feel your uncertainty, and your fear, and this places a demand on my being here and being present. Uh, inside, I feel a kind of rigidity. Uh, I think I'm trying to say to you . . .

Fritz: Are you aware that you're always saying I think, I'm trying. Could you tell us what you're aware of?

Don: (Sigh) I'm aware of a sense that I'm becoming like concrete. Sort of setting.

Fritz: Sort of.

Don: Like I am setting. Moving towards rigidity. Everything is still. (Pause, Claire looks at Fritz)

Fritz: What do you want from me?

Claire: (Turns back to Don) Um, I feel . . .

Fritz: What do you want from me?

Claire: Well, I was going to start to speak to him, and uh, I guess I was checking with you.

Fritz: You're checking up on me.

Claire: No, I didn't feel that way.

Fritz: Mmmmm?

Claire: I guess, guidance that I was doing the right thing.

Fritz: Could you tell him the same thing?

Claire: I don't like to tell him the same thing—that I'm looking to him for guidance. But I realize my attitude has implied that. I was going to say that I felt resentful that you became rigid when you felt that I was fearful that I can handle my own feelings, and it made me feel quite strong.

Fritz: Okay, let's have couple number two. I don't want to go any deeper yet. I just want to get the first idea of how much communication is there. Your name is?

Russ: Russ.

Penny: Penny. (Pause)

Fritz: Look, once more. The experiment is so simple. I don't mind you being somewhat rigid about it. First, what am I aware of in regard to myself—what am I aware of in regard to you. If this is too much of a task, please say so, then we have to deal with your difficulty in comprehending such a simple request.

Russ: I'm aware that I'm afraid of what you're going to say. (Pause) I can listen.

Fritz: Your turn, Penny.

Penny: I'm aware of the tenseness in my chest. I'm aware of your looking at me very intensely, that you seem to want me to carry the ball. (Laughs)

Fritz: Is this what you're aware of or is this what you think?

Penny: It's what I think.

Russ: I'm aware that I want you to do that. I want you to get me primed, and I'm aware that I'm . . .

Fritz: Are you aware of what your hands are doing? Now, please try the most difficult task of all. Stick to the obvious. It's obvious that you just made this movement with your head.

It's obvious that you're holding your hands this way. It's obvious that you're nodding your head. Try to get to the difficult task of simplicity.

Russ: I'm aware that I'm trying too hard. I'm trying to relax and trying to hold on at the same time.

Fritz: How are you doing this trying?

Russ: With my hands, and my body's rigid. I'm rigid.

Fritz: (To Penny) Now, what are you aware of there?

Russ: Your hands are saying something. Quietly, softly—you're leaning away from me.

Fritz: Now, the first time that he sees, yah? Now go back to yourself, again. What happens in this interval? Are you rehearsing?

Russ: I think so.

Fritz: So tell her how you rehearse.

Russ: I want to say the right thing. I want to do the right thing. I'm not really sure where I'm at with you, all the time I'm not sure that I'm really hearing you, or whether I'm projecting.

Fritz: You talk, Penny.

Penny: I'm aware of the pressure on my right arm. I'm aware that I'm leaning away from you. I feel myself pulling back away from you. I'm afraid of being sucked in.

Fritz: Your turn, Russ.

Russ: (Pause) I want to suck you in.

Fritz: Are you aware of that? Um, another difficult moment—we are very much inclined to do this mind-fucking bit. Talk, talk, talk—just tell us your response, what you actually feel. You feel yourself sitting on the chair, you feel yourself nodding your head, so be simple.

Russ: Fine. I feel I'm putting a lot of pressure on my right arm.

Fritz: That's it. See, this I believe.

Russ: I'm holding myself back with my left.

Fritz: Now we get to a bit of reality. Now, open

your eyes again. What do you see? What do you hear?

Russ: I guess, I can't come all the way out.

Fritz: Okay. Thank you. Next couple. (Pause) It's unbelievable that people who live together have so little communication between them, once you get to the brass tacks level—to the real level.

Ann: I'm aware of . . .

Fritz: What's your name?

Ann: Ann.

Bill: Bill.

Fritz: Ann; Bill.

Ann: I'm aware of my heart pounding, and that I'm aware of the, sort of, sitting in this chair, sort of, very solidly back in the chair, with my arms kind of propped on each side. And I'm aware of you looking very, uh, intently into my eyes. (Pause) And breathing more, uh, quickly, uh, at least I'm aware of your breathing.

Fritz: Bill.

Bill: My heart is thumping. And I'm leaning a little bit on my left arm. The thing is, I seem to totally, to be settling, settling down, coming to the center. (Pause) And I see you, Ann. I see your face as being soft, but a bit tense. And I see your right shoulder, just very slightly tensed and . . .

Fritz: Are you aware of what your eyes are doing?

Bill: They're wandering around.

Fritz: What are you avoiding when you look at her?

Bill: I'm trying to find myself, right now, I think. And I'm not prepared to deal with what's out there until I come back here.

Fritz: Very good. Close your eyes and withdraw. So, this is a very good example—he's not ready to cope, so he needs more time for withdrawing into himself, and to get support from within. So, what do you experience?

Bill: I experience a need, really, to re-adjust my position and to come right down to the center . . . to come back to, um . . .

Fritz: Take your time. When you're ready to come back, come back.

Bill: I'm experiencing some tension in my knees right now. My legs are shaking a bit.

Fritz: Now, let's integrate these two things. Tell her of your inner experiences.

Bill: I'm feeling a bit of trembling now—I'm a little bit uncertain, nervous, twitchy. (Pause) That's changing now.

Fritz: Ah, you notice what happened. From the conceptual, from the intentional, to the attention, to using this experience as a means of communication. Now he doesn't hide his trembling anymore, he gives it to her. And, as soon as you express yourself genuinely, all discomfort disappears. Or, if you feel uncomfortable you can be sure that you're not in honest communication. Okay, thank you.

Gestalt Prayer

This time I want to start, so to say, at the end of the road. Namely with the Gestalt prayer. I would like you to repeat after me and then I would like some couples to see what they can do with these sentences. Now the Gestalt prayer goes something like this: I am I,

Group: I am I,

Fritz: And you are you.

Group: And you are you.

Fritz: I'm not in this world to live up to your expectations.

Group: I'm not in this world to live up to your expectations.

Fritz: And you're not in this world to live up to mine.

Group: And you're not in this world to live up to mine.

Fritz: I is I,
Group: I is I,
Fritz: And you is you.
Group: And you is you.
Fritz: Amen. (Laughter) So, let's have some couples and see what they can do with this Gestalt prayer. (Don and Claire come forward)

Don: Um, you expect me home every night at 3:00 and I'm not gonna be there. (Laughs)

Claire: I don't think I expect that. (Laughs)

Don: Um, I think you do.

Claire: I like to feel I share with you certain things—I sometimes feel you're unwilling to share with me. (Pause) I really am trying to be I, and perhaps I don't let you be you enough. (Clears throat) And the more I try to be I, it doesn't seem to always be enough. It seems I have to be that much more. I never seem to catch up with myself.

Don: (Pause) Um, well, if you're feeling a bit, a bit bad about being yourself, and dissatisfied, that's not my problem.

Claire: Then I guess I worry about what you are, perhaps, too much, in addition to (laughs) worrying about where I am.

Don: If you worry about where I am or what I'm doing . . .

Fritz: Yah, now you see what happens. I gave them a task, and immediately the whole Gestalt approach is thrown out of the window. No more talking about the present experience. No more talking about really what is happening. Instead of really communicating on the level on which they are, they start the famous mind-fucking game, which finally ends up in the blaming game. Let's try again, but at the same time, stay with the now. Always tell the other person your reactions and your thoughts. And the simplest way is to think aloud. As a matter of fact, I guarantee each one of you to become a writer within six weeks, if they can sit down on the typewriter and write out exactly each word as they think it. It would go like this—Fritz told me I could become a writer in six weeks. I don't believe it. I think it's all rubbish. Now what shall I write now? I don't know. I'm stuck, nothing comes. To hell with Fritz. (Laughter) You know, if you're exact and honest, each word just appears in your thinking, because thinking is nothing but sub-vocal talking. What we usually do in our so-called thinking is that we rehearse; we try out and let it go through a censor, and then let only those sentences out as they are required to manipulate the other person. We usually produce sentences to hypnotize the other person—to persuade, to deceive, to convince. Very seldom do we speak in order to express ourselves and bring ourselves forward. The result is that all those encounters between human beings usually are sterile. Usually either mind-fucking or manipulation. So, try again, on this basis, to say what the basis of the expectation is. Then, to save time, say I experience now, this, and so on. And don't rehearse. The therapy situation is a safe emergency situation. You can try out all kinds of things and realize that the world doesn't fall to pieces if you're angry or if you're honest. And then you go out into the world and you might get some more confidence. You see that people appreciate honesty much more than you expect them to. Sure, many people will be offended and peeved, but those are mostly the people that are not worthwhile cultivating as friends.

Claire: I see that you seem apprehensive and you're clutching at your fingers, like searching for something to say.

Don: Um, you, um, I, uh, I've noticed that too, that I'm pinching myself, and I've been wondering why I've been doing this—fiddling with myself.

Fritz: Yah. Now what a person does on a non-verbal level usually applies to that person who is implicitly or explicitly in the thing. If he pinches himself, it means he wants to pinch her. (Pause) We usually do to ourselves what we want to do to others. So pinch her.

Don: (Laughs, leans over and pinches Claire on the leg) That was a gentle pinch. (Laughter) Maybe I think there's some truth in that because, uh, I was saying to you just before we came up here, you should tell that dream.

Claire: You were pushing me.

Don: I was being a pusher, and I think it was none of my business what you did, because I also have a dream.

Claire: Yeah.

Fritz: Another most important non-verbal expression is the mask a person is wearing. Now you notice she is grimacing all the time and he is always wearing the serious professor face. Talk a bit to each other about your faces. What do you see? What do you observe?

Don: Well, I like your face, but it does smile a lot, and uh, I think it reflects an uneasiness and you're trying to do something to people with your smile.

Fritz: He's interpreting her.

Claire: Well I agree, uh . . .

Fritz: And every interpretation, of course, is an interference. You tell the other person what they think and what they feel. You don't let them discover themselves.

Claire: Well I think it's quite true. I, uh, mask how I feel by smiling. And uh, I don't like to hurt people or maybe be too honest. (Smiles) Maybe that's it. Um, I find you look quite steadily and honestly—slightly quizzical.

Fritz: How don't you like to hurt him? Tell him, I don't like to hurt you, by being, so and so.

Claire: Uh, maybe by being honest. (Laughs)

Showing that maybe I'm too dependent or, uh, wanting something that you're unwilling to give.

Fritz: You see, when she stops grimacing she can be quite beautiful.

Don: (Pause) You are beautiful.

Claire: (Laughs) That's really . . . (sigh) that stops the conversation. (Laughs)

Fritz: A sentence which I would like you to use—let's call them gimmicks for the time being. Two gimmicks I would like to introduce here. One is, be very honest with where you stand. Like, I'm stuck, I don't know what to say now. You embarrass me. It's very simple if you're aware of yourself, then just to make that statement; that immediately produces some kind of reaction and some communication. The other is, to translate the famous projection screen, 'it' into I or you. 'It' takes all the responsibility. (Pause) Okay, let's take the next couple, who was number two? (Russ and Penny go to the hot seat) So start also with the Gestalt prayer and then see what you can do with it. You say this to him and you say this to her.

Penny: I expect you to work. You expect me to work. (Laughs) I expect you to be interested in my interests. You expect me to forget mine.

Fritz: You notice the smirk that came up in her? Just keep your eyes and ears open.

Russ: (Pause) I expect you to be interested in my interests. (Pause) I am blank. (Pause) I expect you to communicate to me but I don't expect myself to communicate to you. (Pause) Something like that. (Sigh)

Penny: I expect you to have some of the answers and you expect me to have all of them.

Russ: I expect you to have children. I expect you to be a good mother.

Fritz: I can't see from here whether you're looking at her. Say this again and look at her.

Russ: I expect you to be a good mother . . . to me. (Laughs, laughter in the room) I expect you don't want to be that.

Penny: I know you expect that.

Russ: I expect you to give me hell at times in that respect. And, I expect that until I stop wanting that, I expect your support in that respect.

Fritz: Now let's work a little bit on this. Put that mother you want—the wife-mother—in that chair, and talk to her.

Russ: I want your support. I want your love. I want your guidance.

Fritz: Okay, now be this. Change seats and give him all he wants. Give him support, guidance, love, cuddling the tit, uh, the whole works.

Russ: (Laughs, shakes head) That's not my role.

Fritz: Say this to him.

Russ: That's, that's not my role. I'm not supposed to do that. I'm . . .

Fritz: Fake it. (Laughter) At least, I expect you to have an image of what you want. What is important is that many people still carry their parents with them. Need a mother and so on, even sometimes if they are fifty or sixty, and they do this in order to maintain their status as a child. It's part of their reluctance to grow up. So, be the mother. Give him what he wants. He . . .

Russ: I don't know how.

Fritz: Okay, change seats. Tell the mother how, tell that mother, wife, what you want.

Russ: (Pause, then kicks hassock across the room; goes and fetches it, sits down. Sighs, looks at empty chair)

Fritz: What do you experience now?

Russ: Animosity. Anger.

Fritz: You don't sound angry. You don't look Jewish. (Laughter) But say this to that mother.

Russ: I'm angry at you. I want your love and attention, but I feel I can't get it.

Fritz: Okay. Now, again. Take that seat and give him love and attention. Russ, I love you, I give you all the love and attention you want.

Russ: (Pause) Do you, you know I love you, son. But you have to be a man. You can't do those things. You have to stand on your own feet. You have to be the man in the family.

(Changes seats) Mom, I'm not a man. I'm a little boy. I want the things a little boy wants.

Fritz: Yah. Now, you see, here is where the dream work comes in. He started on this same problem in his dream. The road that has to support him. It's, uh, let's call it more individual therapy—individual growth involved—then he can work it out with her. Okay, go back. Now, can you remember the Gestalt prayer? Can you say it again?

Penny: (Sigh) I expect your support.

Fritz: No sweetie, you might need a pair of new ears. This is one of the cases of lacking ears. She probably talks. And people who talk mostly have no ears. They expect other people to have ears but they themselves are deaf. (To Russ) Can you remember the Gestalt prayer?

Russ: I remember the first part of it.

Fritz: Say it to her.

Russ: I am I. You are you. I can't remember any more of it.

Fritz: Could you say I don't want to remember?

Russ: No, I do want to remember. Well. (Pause)

Fritz: What do you experience now?

Penny: Ah, I feel kinda dumb.

Fritz: What do you feel about her not remembering?

Russ: She is not dumb.

Fritz: When you don't remember, you're dumb. If she doesn't remember, she's not dumb.

Russ: (Laughs) She's kind of uptight right now.

Fritz: Mmmhmm.

Russ: That doesn't help memory too much. (Sigh, long pause)

Fritz: Maybe give him, serve him chicken soup. (Laughter)

Russ: (Clears throat, pause) Uh, I can't, I can't put forth.

Fritz: (To Penny) You're looking at me. What do you want from me? As soon as I asked you, your eyes went away from me. What's going on?

Penny: I, (laughs) all right, I'm not seeing anything.

Fritz: So we are probably here at an impasse. The impasse—you get confused, dumb, go on a merry-go-round, repeating the whole thing all over, trying to get out of it, but you're stuck. And the two really seem to be stuck with their expectations. But once they have established the script, this goes on for ever and ever and ever, if you don't get through the impasse. And this is—let's call it my pride. I think in Gestalt therapy, for the first time, that we're capable of going through the impasse. If you don't get through the impasse, all you're interested in is keeping the status quo. Whether in therapy, whether you're in a conflict within your marriage, all you achieve is retaining the status quo; at best change therapists, change marriage partners, change the nature of the inner conflicts, but the nature of this being torn apart remains a lifescript—remains unchanged though the actors might replace each other. Thank you. So, couple number three. (Turns to Bill) So tell her the Gestalt prayer.

Bill: I am I. And you are you. And I will have no expectations of you. And I will accept no expectations of me from you. (Pause) I am I. And you are you. Amen.

Fritz: Now you say it to him.

Ann: I am I. And you are you. I will have no expectations of you. And you can have no expectations of me. I am I and you are you.

Bill: That's great. (Sigh) That's the way the world is. It operates just beautifully that way.

Ann: I don't feel it's really that way for me. (Laughs) I feel that it's, it would be, you know, that . . .

Bill: Right now, it's not that way for you. (Pause) How is it now for you?

Ann: I feel, uh, I feel that you've, uh, um, come to me, and I haven't really come to you. So, I, I feel, in a sense, I feel an expectation, that, you know . . .

Bill: You feel I'm making a demand. Sort of saying, turn here.

Ann: Yes. When you say, it's great, that this is, um, this is some sort of demand that I feel, you know, it's great too. (Starts to cry)

Bill: Would, would you believe that it, if I said that was just the way I felt, when I said, when I say that now?

Ann: Say it. Say it again.

Bill: (Sigh) I am I. And you are you. (Pause) And I can't say now that that's great because some tension has come into here.

Fritz: You see, it's easy to repeat a sentence. And to hypnotize yourself into the belief that the sentence is a reality.

Ann: I, I feel, um, (crying) ah, this is, no feeling that I have with you, that kind of, you know, that some, that you sort of felt that something was really good for you and I sort of put a damper on it because I didn't, uh, sort of build it up or, you know, sort of give what you want, sort of, you know, sort of fly away with it. How did you feel then, you know, when Fritz said that . . .

Bill: I just, uh, I just experienced, uh, some tension in here. When, I suppose when you asked me to say it again, then I felt, uh, some kind of compulsion to say it. And, uh, then it wasn't real.

Ann: How did you feel about me then?

Bill: (Pause) I, at the time, then, remembering back now, I felt, I felt patient.

Ann: Condescending. Patient. What do you mean by patient?

Bill: I didn't feel that you should do anything. And, you know, I often do. Then I didn't. The should factor wasn't there. (Pause) Now, you've found out, where I'm sort of at. Now, now where are you at?

Ann: Mmmm. I, uh, I'm just trying to find myself again. I think I, sort of, well, that was thinking.

Fritz: Are you stuck?

Ann: Uh, yes, I am.

Fritz: So, describe the experience of being stuck.

Ann: (Pause) I feel that I'm sort of, uh, sitting here, somewhat immobilized, waiting for something to unstuck me. (Pause) Uh, I feel some, uh, tingling around my eyes.

Fritz: How do you feel stuck?

Ann: I, I feel an unwillingness to move. (Pause) Uh, I feel that I don't really know where I am. (Pause) On the other hand, I don't just want you to (laughs) tell me. I want to find . . .

Bill: My, you know, my temptation is to, to find it for you, or something. (Pause)

Fritz: We can roughly categorize speech into three different categories. One is aboutism, or signs, or gossip—when you talk about another person or about your feelings, never touching the heart of the matter. And this is what is usually also done in group therapy—people talking with each other or at each other. The second category is not quite explicit here, but is the basis of the bad communications. This is shouldism, or moralism. Always being dissatisfied with what is. You should be different; you should do this; I should do this; should, should, should. And this is identical with expectation. I expect you to listen to my commands and demands.

And the third is is-ism, or existentialism. This is what it is. A rose is a rose is a rose. I am stuck now. I feel I want something from you. I don't know what to do. I would like to say to Fritz, to hell with you. I am bored. Whatever it is. So let's try a bit more on a more honest level of shouldism. Tell each other what you should do and you tell him what he should do and what you should do and so on.

Ann: You should, um, you should be there when I'm lost. But (crying) not show me the way. Just be there. You shouldn't give me any direction.

Fritz: Now this is a very important form of manipulation. Playing the crybaby. I notice this is one of your favorite roles.

Ann: Mmmhhmm.

Fritz: Instead of making him cry, you cry. Crying is a very well known form of aggression. Look what you're doing to me, say this to him. Look what you're doing to me.

Ann: Look what you're doing to me.

Fritz: Again.

Ann: Look what you're doing to me.

Fritz: Louder.

Ann: Look what you're doing to me.

Fritz: Louder.

Ann: (Crying) Look what you're doing to me.

Fritz: Now you begin to communicate. Now he should feel guilty and down in the shit house. Don't you?

Bill: No. (Laughter)

Fritz: And so, start again. (Laughter)

Ann: (Laughing) He's been through this too many times.

Bill: I think you wonder what I'm doing to you.

Fritz: You're not living up to her expectations. You're a very naughty boy. (Laughter)

Couples No. 1

Each one of us has this lifescript which he wants to actualize. Now, sometimes you meet a person who apparently fits into your lifescript, and then you marry this person, and then comes the great moment when you are stuck with each other. Now, this idea of being stuck is quite known. What is less known is that no marriage can be improved or made to function well until you are fully attentive to the way you are stuck. Some of you have seen the picture "The Woman in the Dunes." You remember how this man wanted to get out of being stuck and the more he tried the more he got into quicksand. And we have experienced the same with the war in Viet Nam. The more we tried to get out, the more we got stuck in the quicksand of that whole thing there. And, I pride myself to have overcome what the Russians call the sick point. The Russians have seen that in the center of each neurosis there is a sick point, and they are satisfied to realize they can't get beyond the sick point. So leave the sick point where it is and organize the energies around it, so to say, and sublimate them. I believe that we can get through that impasse provided we pay full attention to the way we are stuck. Again, it's not pleasant. It's much nicer to play the blaming game. You should be different from what you are, and so on, rather to realize that one is stuck and find out how one is stuck and to work from there. So, I like to give at least a superficial picture of how you married or in love people are stuck with each other. So, I would like each couple to come forward and spend a few seconds or minutes with me. Your name is?

Russ: Russ.

Penny: Penny.

Fritz: Russ and Penny. So, you tell Penny, Penny I'm stuck with you. Tell her how you are stuck with her.

Russ: Tell her how I'm stuck with her? I'm stuck with you. How I'm stuck with her?

Fritz: It's okay. (Laughter) Now, we'll talk later on about the holes in a personality. Apparently, Russ hasn't got ears. So, I'm going to be helpful. I say, tell her how you are stuck with her.

Russ: (Pause)

Fritz: Okay, Penny, can you tell him how you are stuck with him?

Penny: I'm stuck with you. You're a lazy ass. I'm stuck with your idleness, I'm stuck with your greatness, I'm stuck with your motorcycle. (Laughter)

Fritz: Okay Russ, you talk now.

Russ: I'm stuck with your bitchiness (Laughter), I'm stuck with your, sometimes, extravagance, I'm stuck with your practicality.

Fritz: How do you dream? (Pause) What did I say?

Russ: Couldn't hear.

Fritz: (To Penny) What did I say?

Penny: How do you dream?

Fritz: Can you tell us?

Penny: How I dream? Colorfully, vividly.

Russ: Hazily. I usually don't remember.

Fritz: Okay, let's have the next couple.

Mark: Do you want me to start? (Pause) I'm stuck with your dreams, your wholehearted impetuousness, your poetic qualities, your dreams.

Fritz: By dreams, you mean daydreams or night-dreams?

Mark: (Pause)

Jenny: I'm stuck with you not wanting me to do certain things, your criticism. I'm stuck with your fears, I'm stuck with your conservatism.

Fritz: What about your nightdreams? Do you have dreams at night?

Jenny: Yes. You're looking for a repeating pattern in my dreams?

Fritz: Yes, possibly.

Jenny: I'm not conscious of a repeated pattern, but I do have dreams.

Fritz: How about you?

Mark: I was thinking of a dream that she has quite often. I was thinking of the one—the stairwell and there's no stairs. The threatened figure, that turned out to be something like the . . .

Jenny: Well, my dreams are usually about adventures and doing things; things that are somewhat harrowing.

Fritz: Okay, thank you. Let's have the next couple.

Sylvia: I feel like I have to invent things. I can't think of anything.

Ken: I get stuck with your pushiness, your, sometimes, aggressions, your sloppy generalities, and your demands.

Fritz: What about your dreams? Do you have nightdreams? Repetitive nightdreams?

Sylvia: You mean the same one all the time?

Fritz: Something similar. Yah.

Sylvia: No. All different.

Fritz: And you?

Ken: Uh, just one I had not too long ago. It was, I kept, I seem to forget.

Fritz: Okay.

Ken: It involved Sylvia and I climbing a mountain with my cat (Laughter) and there was a railway track going up the mountain and I couldn't understand how the train would go straight up. And we were climbing very high up and my cat would keep jumping off the ledge and then it would be up again and keep jumping down . . .

Fritz: Okay.

Judy: Why don't you start?

Nick: I don't feel stuck at all, I'm afraid.

Fritz: Say this to her.

Nick: I don't feel stuck at all.

Judy: Well I'm stuck.

Fritz: Tell him how you're stuck.

Judy: Well, he knows that I'm stuck, but I, I mean there aren't specific ways that I can say it, because I feel that he is a stuck person, in the sense that everything in him is blocked in. And so, I can't say that I'm stuck by certain things about him because I can be objective and say, I like you, but in our relationship, you're stuck because nothing comes out. But if I want something I always have to go in and get it.

Fritz: How do you dream?

Nick: I dream very infrequently and when I do I can usually remember in a sort of semiconscious state. When I first wake up, I can remember it very vividly, but never afterwards.

Fritz: And you?

Judy: I dream a lot and a mood repeats itself in my dreams although the circumstances always change. I have very elaborate sets, but the same moods.

Fritz: Okay, thank you.

Bill: I feel I'm stuck with your, sometimes, inconfidence, with your sort of mucking up my environment, so to speak. Moving things around, cumbersome ways, really. I feel I'm tripping over them, sometimes.

Fritz: And you? Your name is?

Ann: Ann. There's a lot of little things that I feel stuck at the time with you, but the main thing is a whole game thing, that we play, and there's all sorts of little things in you that annoy me when we're doing this, you know, things like, well, mostly things that I feel put on me . . . I become the sort of guardian of your prison, and I become the person who sort of limits you.

Fritz: Now that's an interesting remark—I become the guardian of your prison—which makes it immediately suspicious that he might need a prison in his lifescript. So, you select somebody who will provide the prison. His lifescripts are really the most intricate things. It's unbelievable—anybody would just write down a drama or comedy, and wouldn't believe that he could use all these things himself. What's your dream like?

Ann: I dream a lot and I remember a lot. I have two that recur.

Fritz: And you, Bill?

Bill: I dream, I think more occasionally. There's sort of a repeated dream. It's a freedom dream.

Fritz: Good. Fine. Prison—freedom. (Laughter) So, the next couple.

Dick: Fireaway.

Julie: I'm stuck with your irritability, your impatience, your condescending attitude.

Dick: I'm stuck with sort of, us, and um, sort of the way that I need you to stop me from carrying my impetuousness to an extreme, where I would . . .

Fritz: He needs a power brake.

Dick: Is that where it's at? (Laughter)

Fritz: Okay, thank you. Any more couples? How many couples do we have so far?

Question: I think Nick is just so used to the word "stuck" and the connotations that you're trying to find out the bad things about it or the wrong things about it, when, you know, we're used to that word.

Answer: I think Fritz did it. You, I immediately resented you for saying that fantastic generalization about people being stuck. It's like something you've thought out and seen in a lot of couples, and therefore it was true for everyone, and I felt bound by your cliche. I can say I resent things but I, I couldn't say I'm stuck with them.

Question: Doesn't that mean that we're bound by semantics?

Answer: Well, maybe, maybe. Well, I choose to be

stuck and therefore I'm not stuck, you know. I mean, I choose to be. (Laughter)

Question: The word stuck implies that you want to get out of it.

Answer: Maybe that's just a semantic problem.

Question: Well, is mankind going to be stuck with marriage for a long time to come or can we find a better institution?

Fritz: Would any of these couples here think of going to a marriage counselor or look for any help in their marriage? Well, then, I think that the whole thing is out of gear. You can make a film on marriages, only the main idea is how to help dead marriages to improve. Well, what you might do is to try to improve the marriage as though you're not tearing on your chains. (Laughter) Okay, next couple. (Ellen and Gordon come forward) Now the first thing you notice here, and the essential thing in Gestalt therapy, is, the non-verbal is always more important than the verbal. Words lie and persuade; but the posture, the voice, the non-verbal behavior is true. Have you noticed? First thing is a closed posture. What's your name again?

Ellen: Ellen.

Fritz: Ellen. You notice Ellen is a closed system. Legs are closed, hands are closed. Very difficult to communicate with a closed system. So, will you do me a favor?

Ellen: Mmmhhmm.

Fritz: See what would happen if you were to open up. How does this feel?

Ellen: Easier.

Fritz: So, will you talk to Gordon and tell him how you're stuck with him?

Ellen: I don't know. I haven't seen Gordon for a long time.

Fritz: Gordon, will you tell Ellen how you're stuck with her?

Gordon: I don't feel stuck with you now.

Ellen: I didn't understand your word. Oh, I thought you said stuck and I was trying to understand it.

Fritz: Stuck. Stuck. (Laughter)

Ellen: I don't feel stuck wth Gordon—I feel, I feel myself.

Fritz: So, there are no complaints in your marriage?

Ellen: Uh, well, there have been.

Fritz: But there are no more.

Ellen: Well, because we aren't living, we aren't living together.

Fritz: Then you're not stuck with each other. (Laughter) Do you have any fantasies about coming together again?

Ellen: I don't think I do, anymore.

Fritz: What about your position, Gordon?

Gordon: I feel there's something incomplete. We've just sort of agreed to be apart, but there are still the children to think about and there are still, I'm still concerned in some way.

Fritz: What about you?

Ellen: Well, I'm concerned, but that doesn't necessarily mean being together.

Fritz: So what do you want from him? You say there are certain things that should still be discussed. What about your position? Where do you stand?

Ellen: I think there's plenty that could be discussed. But I don't see, I haven't any particular expectation of, uh, coming together or staying apart, or uh, whatever.

Fritz: Doesn't matter one way or another. I wouldn't say this, 'but!' You probably have a 'but' somewhere on your hands.

Ellen: (Laughs) Maybe you have.

Fritz: There are two killers. One is the sneer or the, let's say, malicious laugh, and the other is the word 'but.' These two are the psychological killers. First say yes. Then comes the but. Boom! There's a little story about it.

Uh, mother says to her daughter, well, he's ugly but he has thirty thousand dollars. And the daughter says, mother, you're so right. He has thirty thousand dollars but he's ugly. (Laughter)

Couples No. 2

Fritz: Well, we've got a new couple here in this group, and I'd like to find out what might happen with the people who have not been initiated into the Gestalt approach. Will you take seats? And your name is?

Irwin: Irwin.

Fritz: Irwin. And yours is?

Nancy: Nancy.

Fritz: Nancy. Would you start out talking for a couple of minutes to each other?

Irwin: Hello.

Nancy: How are you?

Irwin: Fine. (Pause) How'd you like lying in the sun?

Nancy: It was very restful. I enjoyed it.

Irwin: Yeah. (Pause) It's hard to talk to you, in a way. I don't know what to say.

Nancy: Well, maybe you don't have to say anything.

Irwin: Um, I feel sort of, that I should be saying something. But I don't know what to say. Uh, first time I've looked this long into your eyes. I haven't looked this long into your eyes. Uh . . .

Fritz: So may I have your single opinion? What's your impression of your marriage?

Irwin: Uh, some ways good, some ways, not so good. Uh, in the way that it's good, there's sometimes a warmth between us, there's a cuddliness. Uh, where it's no good, or maybe not so good, is sometimes I play the master and she plays the nigger. Sort of a master-slave relationship.

Fritz: Well, you see the topdog-underdog game is not confined to the struggle within. We very often like to project it, act it out, and then we only are aware of the topdog in ourself, not the underdog, because the underdog always is there. And vice versa. Nancy, what's your . . .

Nancy: Well, I think lots of times I play underdog and then I become resentful when, and then, I guess I like to play topdog, too, to a degree, in a way.

Fritz: Yah. Now, when you work with each other, we're going to play some marriage games. And nothing you say will be taken as evidence against you. It means, if you promise something here, or you say something, it only holds good for within this situation here. So, I want to say this so that it might be able to mobilize your fantasy. So, let's first play the evocation game. When we address somebody, we want this person to be there; we always evoke the other person. With darling, or you son of a bitch, or sweetie, or Jesus Christ. (Laughter) Now, I would like to play this evocation game in this way. You say Nancy, and wait a moment, repeat it again. And you nod your head, or shake your head, and see whether he can reach you simply with evoking your name.

Irwin: Okay. (Sigh) Nancy. . . . . . Nancy . . . . . . Nancy (Pause) Stink.

Nancy: (Laughs)

Irwin: Asshole.

Fritz: Just stick to the name Nancy.

Irwin: Mmhhmm. Okay. Nancy . . . . . . Nancy . . . . . . Nancy . . . . . . Nancy . . . . . . Nancy . . . . . . Nancy! Nancy . . . . . . Nancy . . . . . . Nancy.

Fritz: Now, let's reverse it. See whether you can evoke him.

Nancy: Irwin. (Clears throat) Irwin.

Fritz: (To Irwin) Can you shake your head or nod your head, so that . . .

Irwin: Yeah. First time I thought you, you got to me. Second time . . . (Shakes head)

Nancy: Irwin . . . . . . Irwin . . . . . . Irwin . . . . . . Irwin.

Fritz: I notice, each time she calls you, you're looking away. Well, a lot is going on, just simply with these two names. Did you feel how much you experienced during this simple game? This is the best test of communication. Now, let's play the resentment game. You say, Nancy, I resent this and this in you, and you say a sentence, Irwin, I resent this in you. So, play resentment Ping-Pong.

Irwin: Okay. (Sigh) Yeah. I resent that you don't keep the house as orderly as I'd like it to be.

Nancy: I resent that you want me to keep house the way your mother keeps house.

Irwin: Uh, I resent that you, uh, sometimes don't understand what I'm feeling. You don't feel along with me.

Nancy: I resent that you demand me to feel along with you.

Fritz: You notice what happens—she just hits the board again. Will you now say half a dozen sentences of I resent this.

Nancy: Okay, right. I resent, uh, I resent that you're always nagging at me.

Irwin: Mmmm . . .

Fritz: No, just give us some more resentment.

Nancy: Oh me, okay. I resent that, uh, somehow you make me feel guilty. I resent that you don't spend more time with me and the children at times. I resent that you don't encounter me at times. Uh . . .

Irwin: Uh, I resent when I'm angry at you, that you put sometimes, put your hands in the air, and you go away yelling or screaming, and not letting me, well, I don't know, get angry. But I resent that you put your hands in your ears when I'm angry at you.

Fritz: All right, now let's do the same with appreciation.

Irwin: Uh, okay. When I call you, I appreciate that when I call you that sometimes you're there. I appreciate your holding me sometimes and giving me a nice feeling of warmth, a nice feeling of cuddliness. I appreciate, sometimes, your ideas.

Nancy: And I appreciate your strength, and your, uh, givingness, at certain times, when I need it. Uh, I appreciate your sense of humor. And I appreciate your bringing home ideas to share. I appreciate, uh, some of, (Pause) your spontaneity.

Irwin: I appreciate your daredevilness. You're willing to take more risks than myself. In a way.

Fritz: Ya. Let's go back to the resentment game. Start resenting again, and follow up your resenting with a should. Behind every resentment there is a demand.

Irwin: Mmhhmm. Uh, you should, uh, sense that I sometimes need you. I think sometimes you guess what I'm saying before I say it or sometimes to sort of make it easy for me to say what I want to say.

Fritz: Can you reinforce this? Say you should do this, you should do that. Make your demands very explicit so that she knows where she stands.

Irwin: Okay. Uh, the other day I had sort of a run in with one of the teachers at the school. And, uh, I was feeling bad; I didn't seem to come off good with him and I was feeling hurt. And when I went to the bedroom, uh, you should have sensed my hurt and responded to this hurt.

Fritz: Now you give him a resentment, Nancy. Make a demand.

Nancy: Uh, I resent sometimes that you demand so much time that I don't have time to do the other household things that need doing or to take care of little things. You become too hurt over my, uh, doing anything but paying attention to you. I think you should enjoy me while I'm there and then say, be able to say good-bye.

Fritz: Now you give her a demand.

Irwin: Okay. Uh, when I'm feeling closed, don't come over and sort of open me up. Uh, don't just jump at me. I don't know what you could do—perhaps sort of indicate that you're about to come to me. That doesn't make any sense, but, uh, at least don't, uh, when I feel closed don't come into me. Then when I feel open, be open to me. Specifically, sometimes in the morning you'll come over and hug me and I'll feel closed—so don't hug me when I, when you sense I'm closed.

Fritz: Now you demand, Nancy.

Nancy: Um, I don't want to feel so guilty. I don't know whether you make me feel guilty or I make myself feel guilty. But I don't think you're somehow helping the situation. I don't exactly know how to tell you not to make me feel guilty, because that's silly. But, um, I think you get messed up in it somehow.

Fritz: Okay. Next step. He makes a demand on you and you are spiting him. You say, all right, if you want to be closed, I'll come with an axe and break you open. Just get the wildest spite into this. (Laughter)

Nancy: Mmm. Okay.

Fritz: This is the best way to improve marriages, believe it or not.

Irwin: Yeah. This actually happened last week. (Laughter) Uh, I feel like just taking a walk and being by myself and I don't want to walk with you. I feel like walking to the school by myself, and I stay home and I just need a moment of aloneness, and don't come with me. Stay where you are, stay on the couch. And uh, good-bye.

Fritz: Spite him.

Nancy: I feel very furious that, that you're doing that. I'm going to . . .

Fritz: No, no, no. That's not spiting. When you're going to school I'm going to hang onto you . . .

Nancy: Yeah, I'm going to hang onto you.

Fritz: Frustrate him to the gills.

Nancy: I will, I will cry. I will throw a temper tantrum, I will jump up and down, I will say don't go. I will make you feel terribly guilty.

Fritz: You see, now she becomes alive.

Nancy: Uh, yes, right. (Laughter) Uh, I will jump up and down. I will make you feel very guilty by telling you how much you're neglecting me and uh, that you don't, that you really should, that your duty is to stay with me.

Fritz: Okay. Now you give him a demand. And you spite her. And you see how good you are in spiting.

Nancy: Uh, take out the garbage.

Irwin: No, I'm not taking out the garbage. I have to go upstairs and I have to read and, uh, and let's see, I've got a lot of things to do. I'm really too tired. You take out the garbage. Uh, I've got to go down and do some sculpturing. I've got to do something that is more important than taking out the garbage. Uh, I'm not going to do it. You should do it.

Fritz: You make a demand. Spite her again. You notice that she's much better at spiting and you also probably noticed in the beginning that she's the good girl. And behind the good girl and the good boy, there's always the spiteful brat.

Irwin: Uh, let's see, okay. Drive carefully. Now remember, put the clutch all the way in and don't forget you're supposed to be in fourth, not in third. I told you hundreds of times that when we're past thirty five that you put it into fourth.

Fritz: Now spite him.

Nancy: Well, uh, so I won't go over thirty five. So then I won't go into fourth and that'll teach you. (Laughter)

Fritz: Good. Now you make a demand on him.

Nancy: Uh, I would like to go to the symphony, and I know you don't want to go, so I'm going to find some of my friends and go with them.

Irwin: Well, maybe I'll go wih you. And, uh, if the music is not to my liking, I'll make it really difficult for you. I'll tell you how crappy it is, and how modern it is and how shitty it is and I'll indicate that this kind of music is too, uh, too new for me, and I'll make you feel really crummy. I'll indicate that the music is shitty because I know you like music.

Fritz: Now, let's play the compliance game. You make a demand and you exaggerate this compliance.

Irwin: Uh, rub my feet. Would you?

Nancy: Oh, I'll rub your feet. I'll rub them all night long. I'll rub them so hard I can . . . they'll get sore. (Laughter)

Fritz: Make a demand. See if she's capable of complying.

Irwin: Okay. Uh, (Sigh) when I feel bad, when I feel hurt, when something goes wrong at school, can you come up and give me re-assurance, can you tell me that the world is not going to fall apart and that the, uh, that everything is okay?

Nancy: I can try. I can make it. Should I make it absurd?

Fritz: No. I want to test you out whether you're capable at all to be cooperative and suppor-tive and compliant. Or whether you're just a spiteful brat.

Nancy: Um yes, I can come up and, uh, perhaps, um . . .

Fritz: Perhaps. I try. You know the typical language of the underdog. Let me repeat the underdog-topdog behavior in this context. The topdog is the righteous bully. The one who tells the underdog how to behave and so on. Usually straightforward in his demands and commands. The underdog says yeah, I try my best, if I could do it. In other words, the underdog usually wins. The topdog controls and the underdog is in control. Okay, thank you. That's as far as I want to go.

Nancy: Thank you.

Fritz: So, next couple. Your name is?

Marty: Marty.

Susan: Susan.

Fritz: So, I like Marty and you. See how much more we can get into the understanding of spite. We'll start with the resentment game. Let's also start with the evocation game. (Pause)

Marty: Okay. Um, I resent the fact that you don't give me more freedom and you should be willing and able to give me more freedom than you do.

Susan: I resent, uh, not having freedom also. And I resent the feeling of guilt when I do have—take freedom.

Marty: I resent, I resent you when you turn, when you turn off to me. When you pretend to be angry.

Fritz: Tell her you should. Follow up with you should.

Marty: (Sigh) You should, and you should not do this.

Fritz: Say this again.

Marty: And you should not do this?

Fritz: Can you cut out the and?

Marty: You should not do this.

Fritz: Say it again.

Marty: You shouldn't do it.

Fritz: Louder.
Marty: You shouldn't do it!
Fritz: Scream it at her.
Marty: You shouldn't do it!
Fritz: You shouldn't do what?
Marty: You shouldn't, you shouldn't play angry at me when you're not really angry.
Fritz: Now, give him your resentment and make your demands very explicitly.
Susan: I resent when I am truly angry at you—of your walking away and not listening, and you should listen.
Fritz: Just say listen, listen, listen.
Susan: You should listen.
Fritz: Again.
Susan: You should listen.
Fritz: Louder.
Susan: You should listen!
Fritz: Are you aware of what you're doing with your face?
Susan: No.
Fritz: I would like you to verbalize what I see in your face. Tell him, I despise you.
Susan: Tell him I despise him?
Fritz: Yes.
Susan: I despise you.
Fritz: Again.
Susan: I despise you.
Fritz: Can you feel it?
Susan: No.
Fritz: What is this smirk of yours? Let's try another formulation which might be closer—I can't take you seriously.
Susan: I can't take you seriously.
Fritz: Again.
Susan: I can't take you seriously. (Pause)
Fritz: True?
Susan: True.
Fritz: Now. Reinforce this. Elaborate on this.
Susan: I can't take you seriously because you don't want me to take you seriously and you shouldn't do, uh, shouldn't do that and you

shouldn't tell stories in circles. Shouldn't tell me things in circles. (Sigh)

Fritz: What do you experience right now?

Marty: Frustration.

Fritz: Tell her that.

Marty: I feel frustration. I feel a little, as if I don't quite follow what you're trying to say.

Fritz: Could you say, please say, I refuse to follow what you say.

Marty: I refuse to follow what you say.

Fritz: Again.

Marty: I refuse to follow what you say.

Fritz: What's your reaction?

Susan: I believe him.

Fritz: Say this to him.

Susan: I believe you . . .

Fritz: Again, in a louder voice.

Susan: I believe you because, uh, you do that all the time. You turn off your ears.

Fritz: Follow up every one of your sentences with I find you ridiculous.

Susan: I find you ridiculous.

Fritz: Yah. Each sentence from now on. (Pause) What do you experience now?

Marty: I experience a little amusement at, when you told her to add, I find you ridiculous at the end of a sentence.

Fritz: Say this to her.

Marty: I felt a little humor when Fritz said to add ridiculous.

Fritz: What do you experience now?

Susan: I want to ask you why, but you're not supposed to ask why, so how come—which is the same thing.

Fritz: Ask him why.

Susan: Why? (Pause)

Fritz: Before you wanted to ask him, what did you experience?

Susan: I, um, felt truth. I felt that it was true, in being ridiculous, in you being ridiculous, and you know it and that's why you felt funny.

Fritz: (Pause) I would like to try a game with

you. Could you go over there to the door and play Christ on the cross? (Pause) Now you go over and take the nails out. Take him off his cross.

Marty: I have a sword in my side.

Susan: I didn't stick the sword in your side. (Laughter)

Marty: Take it out . . .

Fritz: Can you come down to us mortals now?

Marty: Yes. Okay.

Fritz: Where did you meet? If you could see her for the first time, what would you see?

Marty: A physically attractive girl. (Sigh) Who I don't know yet but, um, I'm interested in getting to know.

Fritz: Now the next thing, I notice all the time that you have no hands. Your hands are still chained to each other. No, no, keep your hands this way. Now talk to her, touch her this way, make love to her this way. See what it feels like if you are that closed with your hands.

Marty: What, uh, what was the matter when you woke up this morning? I noticed that you didn't feel very well.

Susan: My back and my leg hurt from when I fell yesterday.

Marty: Were you surprised when Russ didn't come today?

Susan: Yes.

Fritz: Now, make a round and touch a few of us this way, with your hands like they are locked in handcuffs. Now, can you open your hands and see what it feels like to have hands? That you perhaps may be able to handle people. Can you try to handle her now? Handle or mishandle, whatever you do.

Marty: Your hands are cold.

Fritz: Tell him, I freeze you out.

Susan: I freeze you out . . .

Fritz: Again.

Susan: I freeze you out.

Fritz: Can you feel it?

Susan: No.

Marty: (Pause) I do.

Fritz: Okay, that's as far as I want to go. Now, Gordon and Ellen. We still have a few minutes' time. Could you talk to each other about what happened since the last or first encounter you had here?

Ellen: Here?

Fritz: That was two or three days ago, wasn't it?

Ellen: Yes.

Fritz: Tell him and you tell her, what happened. Try to share your experiences—or have you already discussed it?

Gordon: Not very much. (Pause)

Ellen: Well, I remember after telling you some of the things I resent, uh, realizing that what I was resenting . . . was that I had let some of this happen.

Fritz: Now, give him the post-dated orders—you should have . . .

Ellen: I can't remember what I told him I resented, now.

Fritz: Very convenient. And I think you are lying.

Ellen: I think I can get it. Um, you shouldn't, should never have talked down to me. You should have accepted me as an equal and let me feel.

Fritz: Okay. Let's use this. Now tell him, don't talk down to me, Gordon.

Ellen: Don't ever talk down to me.

Fritz: Louder.

Ellen: Don't ever talk down to me.

Fritz: Say this with your whole body now.

Ellen: Don't ever talk down to me!

Fritz: Again.

Ellen: Don't ever talk down to me!

Fritz: Can you say it more from your guts than from your throat?

Ellen: Don't talk down to me! Just don't! Don't laugh either!

Fritz: Now let's reverse it. You play Gordon. You talk down to him.

Ellen: Why do you always mess around with the hardest things there are to do in the studio—you know, you could be a fine artist and do lots of good things if you didn't always have to be trying the hard things.

Fritz: Go on, give him hell.

Ellen: You're ridiculous. You're always complaining of not getting approved of. And you, you just make it impossible. You're always defeating yourself.

Fritz: Always tell him what he should do.

Ellen: You should stay with one thing. You should really get going on one thing and stay with it—you know, long enough to do something. (Pause) You shouldn't have to feel superior.

Fritz: Can you also say to him, I don't have to feel superior.

Ellen: I don't have to feel superior.

Fritz: What would happen if you couldn't feel superior—wouldn't have to feel superior?

Ellen: I would just feel me.

Fritz: So, could you try it now on him? And let him be as he is. (Pause)

Ellen: Yes, yes.

Fritz: Can you tell him that?

Ellen: I guess that's the way you are, and that's the way you should be then.

Fritz: Do you mean that or is it just to please me?

Ellen: No, I think I mean it. (Pause) I think I mean it because I feel, uh, it doesn't matter as much to me.

Gordon: I don't believe you. It's a put on—a sudden switch. I'm not convinced.

Fritz: Can you try my formulation? You don't fit my lifescript. You should.

Ellen: Me?

Fritz: Yah. Tell him, you don't fit my lifescript. You should be this and that. I don't know what you want from me—what's your lifescript of your husband?

Ellen: You don't fit my lifescript because, uh, you should be willing to be a partner, to share equally. (Pause)

Fritz: Okay. Can you now say a sentence with, Gordon, I appreciate this—whatever you appreciate in him.

Ellen: Oh, I appreciate, uh, the humor, the . . .

Fritz: Talk to him.

Ellen: The excitement . . .

Fritz: And give him resentments.

Ellen: I resent not being able to find myself in that creative art world. I resent it. I still resent it.

Fritz: Can you tell him, he's responsible for your not being able to find yourself?

Ellen: No, I can't really, because I don't believe it.

Fritz: Then, where's the resentment?

Ellen: Well, maybe (Laughs) the resentment was, is going away.

Fritz: Uh huh. Can you get a balance between resentment and appreciation? Maybe by saying thank you. Is there anything you can be grateful for?

Ellen: Oh yes, sure. I'm grateful that my, that uh, that I had a sudden, a really sudden change of course in my life when I met you. And a lot of things about it have been very good. (Pause) I'm especially grateful for the children, and I appreciate some of the many people I've met, mostly because of you.

Fritz: Okay, can you shake hands?

Ellen: Sure.

Memory and Pride

I'm scanning my intellectual material to find what I can give you to continue work on your own. I know some of you had some growth experiences that will stay with you and go on, but I would like to give you some more general ideas about how to work on yourself and on others. To do this we have to talk a little more about the projection material. Most of the alienated part of us is projected—either into dreams or onto the world. Now many people suffer from self-consciousness. Does anyone here? (Laughter) Okay, will you come forward? (Dawn goes to the hot seat. She is a tall, slim young woman about 23.)

Dawn: I felt very tall when I walked across the room, and I feel self-conscious about . . . about that. I . . .

Fritz: Okay. Take that seat. (Points to the empty chair) Now, play the audience.

Dawn: (Pause) You are very big. Uh, you're a bit awkward actually. Um . . .

Fritz: Change seats. Now, watch this. Has anybody noticed when she went up, that she was very big? (Voices dissenting) Not one person. (To Dawn) Isn't that amazing?

Dawn: Um, it's just that when you stand up and everybody is sitting down, it felt like being in Lilliput Land.

Fritz: Pardon?

Dawn: It felt like being in Lilliput Land.

Fritz: Ah, that's different. Now, get up. Now you're the giant and look at us Lilliputians. (Laughter) Talk to us.

Dawn: (In a deep voice) Hello, down there. Don't be afraid of me.

Fritz: Do you still feel self-conscious?

Dawn: I feel like I'm holding in.

Fritz: Where? What?

Dawn: Here. (Indicates pelvis) I'm, I feel like I'm quite powerful but I'm not allowing it to come out.

Fritz: Okay. Take this seat. Tell Dawn, don't let your power come out.

Dawn: Don't let your power come out.

Fritz: Go on, give her the works.

Dawn: Uh, am I to be the power? I'm just the audience.

Fritz: Let's call it your inhibitions. You're your "don't."

Dawn: I won't let your power come out. Uh, listen to me because I'm actually protecting you. What will they think if they know what you think about yourself? (Changes seats) They might be afraid of me.

Fritz: Now can you change 'they' into 'you' and talk, and say this to the audience?

Dawn: You might be afraid of me.

Fritz: Again.

Dawn: You might be afraid of me.

Fritz: Now stand up and say the same sentence as a giant.

Dawn: You *would* be afraid of me. (Sigh) You might not be afraid of me. You might, uh, you might think that that's a silly idea. You might laugh at me.

Fritz: Okay. Laugh at Dawn. (She laughs) Make fun of her.

Dawn: You foolish girl. (Pause) Why can't you just be what you are?

Fritz: Okay, stand up and say this to us. Make fun of us. Tell us how foolish we are.

Dawn: You are all quite foolish, but I . . . I wouldn't tell you that. I wouldn't hurt you by telling you that.

Fritz: Say this again.

Dawn: I wouldn't hurt you by telling you that.

Fritz: Can you do the reverse? Hurt them. Put them in the chair and hurt them. Make *them* cry.

Dawn: You fools. Here looking for answers. Daring to think that there are answers. You all look so silly. You're not going to find out anything this way.

Fritz: Now say this actually to the members of the group.

Dawn: You're not going to find out anything this way. (Looks around at group) And still you smile. (To Marek)

Marek: But I'm finding out. You're finding out a

lot of things about yourself. I share a lot of your feelings about this whole situation and how phony it is. But it's a long road and maybe this is a step on it. (Pause) No smile.

Fritz: (To Dawn) How do you feel now?

Dawn: Um . . . (sniffing) smaller.

Fritz: Okay. I would like you (indicates Marek) to put phoniness in that chair. Talk to phoniness.

Marek: Phoniness is sitting in that chair. (Pause) Phoniness, phoniness. I have to feel out that word. Phoniness, you're going to tell us all where it's all at. You know. You know that we don't know. That we know about fragments. That we know about crying and smiling—that we know about certain facets of ourselves, but you know everything.

Fritz: Play phoniness.

Marek: (Sigh) Well, it's those little phony games that I'm going to play with all your heads, but they just might mean something. It's up to you. I may be phony, but I want you to realize that you're phony, and perhaps . . . hm, I'm being phony myself, right now, because actually, I don't feel . . . yeah, I feel a lot of tension. I'd like to withdraw myself at this point. Phoniness is going to withdraw into itself. (Laughs) Phoniness, I feel a lot of shaking inside. My whole gut is shaking.

Fritz: You think that shaking is phony?

Marek: No. For phoniness it's real. That's where I am right now, is phoniness. So, (Sigh) if I'm going to be phoniness, then I feel really strong.

Fritz: Ya. Now wait a moment, phoniness. I want to make you real, because your support is in your shaking. Can you dance your shakiness?

Marek: (Walks around, shakes his arms) Yes. A little bit of it. Yes. A little bit.

Fritz: So, go back. Talk to phoniness once more.

Marek: (Sigh) I've lost contact with you, phoniness. I like to feel myself. I feel my heart beating. I don't see . . . I see a stool. I feel a pain in my feet from having jumped up. That's a real feeling. And I see people in the room—Gordon, Ann, yourself. You.

Fritz: What happened to your smirk? (Laughs) Now it's back.

Marek: Yeah. Well, I mean, I . . . some smiling may be possible, isn't it?

Fritz: Okay, you notice a beautiful other polarity—phoniness, and the reverse, being real and authentic. Now let's finish up by putting that smirk in the chair. Talk to your smirk.

Marek: Smirk, I don't like you. But, you have crooked teeth behind that, and when they were fixed, you tried to smile. I'd rather see you . . . I'd rather see you than what you had before. It was a snarl. (Explodes, kicks the stool and then throws a chair) Those fucking Hitler's pigs! (Irwin stops him)

Fritz: Okay, sit down. Close your eyes and attend to your breathing.

Marek: (Pause, Marek breathes deeply) I'm five and a half years old. (Crying, then stops) No, I don't believe it. I don't want to go back there.

Fritz: Before you go back, come back to us first. Can you see me?

Marek: Yeah, I can see you.

Fritz: Are you . . . do you really see me?

Marek: Yeah, I see you.

Fritz: You see where you are, in actual timo?

Marek: (Pause) Yeah, I think so.

Fritz: Okay. Now close your eyes. You are five and a half years again. What do you encounter there?

Marek: (Sigh) We're thirty kilometres from Warsaw. They're burning it. They're partisans. There's a fat S.S. man. He's got a big ruddy face. He lifts me on his shoulders. (Sigh) No, no . . .

Fritz: What do you actually see? With your eyes closed. Now this is very important. Listen to me. Do not try to remember. Just be five and a half years of age and tell me what you see, feel, and hear.

Marek: (Pause) I'm five and a half. (Laughs) Playing in a garden with a friend. (Sigh) They're all around. The partisans rob us. The Germans.

Fritz: Do you see it?

Marek: Yeah, I see them. They're . . .

Fritz: What do you see?

Marek: There's three of them. They're coming to the house. It's a big mansion. I've got to . . . I want to go in and warn everybody . . . well, I know, you're not going to make me go back there. Sorry. That's it.

Fritz: Say this to me.

Marek: No. Like, I'm in Canada, man. (Laughs) That's it.

Fritz: You want to preserve that memory. What do you need this memory for?

Marek: To beat myself over the head with.

Fritz: Whom else do you want to beat over the head?

Marek: Everybody. I think I just did it. (Pause)

Fritz: Come back to us again. (Marek looks around the room)

Marek: Well, if I seem hostile to you, it's there, and there's a lot of hatred. There's a lot of hatred for everyone of you, but, maybe there's a lot of love, too. Not much. But there is some.

Fritz: Okay. Close your eyes. Go back again. Take your time machine and be a child again.

Marek: I'm in the corridor of Uka Vitza which is about thirty kilometres from Warsaw. It's . . . I'm in this corridor. There's an old man at the end of this corridor. He's painting. No one can approach him. (Looks at Fritz) You're the old man, Fritz.

Fritz: Look at me. Am I the old man?

Marek: (Laughs) No.

Fritz: Put the old man in that chair and compare

him to me. What are the similarities, what are the differences?

Marek: The similarity is that you, old man, when I was five and a half . . . you are at the end of a hall, and I am approaching you. And Fritz, you seem to be at the end of an avenue of people, and I also am approaching you. You have grey hair and he has grey hair. You're a painter and you paint with everything you do. You're a sculptor of people. And an artist. And he's an artist.

Fritz: And how are we different?

Marek: You speak. He never spoke a word.

Fritz: Say this to him, now.

Marek: You never spoke a word. But, you were always so different because you painted and that's when I started drawing. You taught me how to draw. And I guess (turns to Fritz) you're teaching me something too. (Pause) You are two different people.

Fritz: Can you realize this now?

Marek: Oh, yes.

Fritz: Okay. Now go back to the Germans. To the unpleasantness.

Marek: No.

Fritz: What's your objection?

Marek: I object.

Fritz: What's your objection?

Marek: That happened a long time ago.

Fritz: You're still carrying it with you.

Marek: I'll carry it for a long time, probably.

Fritz: Can you talk to that memory once more? Say, memory, I won't let you go . . . I hug you in my bosom, carry you day and night.

Marek: Memory, I'm going to carry you in my bosom day and night. No, that's not true. No, I guess it . . . (laughs) I'm retreating into phoniness, perhaps.

Fritz: Change seats. Be the memory.

Marek: (Sigh) Marek, you cannot get rid of me . . . I am you. You like me. It makes you feel good. It makes you feel better than everyone else. You suffered, kid. So I'm going to stay with you . . . everybody else had it soft. And you know that's wrong. (Pause)

Fritz: What's going on now?

Marek: I uh, thought—memories—it isn't important now.

Fritz: Say, bye-bye memory.

Marek: See you. (Laughs)

Fritz: Nietzsche once said, memory and pride were fighting. Memory said it was like that and pride said it couldn't have been. And memory gave in. You see, we treat the memory as something belonging to the now. Whether the memory is true or distorted, we still keep it. We don't assimilate it. We keep it as a battleground or a justification for something. Really, we don't need it. So, I think we'll finish up for this morning.

Philosophy of the Obvious

I would like to call Gestalt Therapy the philosophy of the obvious. We take the obvious for granted. But when we examine the obvious a bit closer, then we see that behind what we call obvious, is a lot of prejudice, distorted faith, beliefs, and so on. But in order to get and understand the obvious, we have to first get hold of the obvious, and that is the greatest difficulty. We all want to be clever or hide, or intend to be something worthwhile, and so on.

You noticed what difficulties you all had in dealing with the obvious. A neurotic is simply a person who does not see the obvious. But in order to deal with the obvious, you first must get hold of the obvious. Now, the most obvious factor we encounter in our sphere is the fact that we have two levels of existence—an inner world and an outer world. And the inner world, often called the mind, looks as if it's something different or opposed to the outer world. One of the characteristics of this inner world is its homeopathic way of being.

Homeopathy is a certain branch in medicine, which is considered in very small as being effective. Now, what I mean by the homeopathic way of the mind operating is this: You want to buy a piece of bread so you don't go out across the street to a fur shop and ask for bread. Then next is a bank; you don't go there and ask for bread. No, you rehearse at first. Even if the rehearsing takes a fraction of a second. You skim the possibilities —this is the place where I go to get the bread. So, this bit of fantasy rehearsing saves a lot of work. And we do a lot of this fantasy planning. Now the sane mind is a kind of minute edition of reality. They both click. They are identical on a smaller scale.

The gestalt that forms in our fantasy has to coincide with the gestalt in the outer world in order to come to a conclusion to cope with life—to finish the situation and so on. When there is no connection between the two then you have the person who lives on anastrophic and catastrophic expectation all the time—imagining that he will be rich and famous and so on. Or if you have catastrophic expectation, you imagine all the time that you will be punished, people won't like you. And the lack of checking out, the lack of getting the parallel between the two amounts to the many distortions and real catastrophes in life.

Now there is one region where we are really insane, where we have a real private life of insanity—of an inner life unconnected with the external world, and that is the dream. The dream appears to be real. As long as you dream, you are really in that situation. You really experience this as being your very existence—especially if you are a self-frustrator—then you dream in terms of nightmares. You want to cope with the situation and achieve something—and again and again you frustrate yourself. You prevent yourself from achieving what you want to achieve. But you don't experience this as you're doing it. You experience this as some other power that is preventing you.

Now we started yesterday with the shuttling between being in touch with the external world and getting in touch with yourself. And once you got in touch with yourself, something usually opened up. And if there's a direct connection, direct communication between the self and the world, you function fine—then your potential is available, you can call on your own resources. But if you try to withdraw and you can't withdraw to yourself but just to that nucleus—that psychotic part in ourselves, that fantasy life, like the computer, the conceptualizing, the explaining, the withdrawals to memories, to the past—then you never can get to the true self. As Freud never got to the self—always getting stuck with the ego. What we can do to understand and make full use of the dreams is to realize that this inner world of dreams is also our lifescript, and it's a much more explicit way of our lifescript.

Just as in our everyday life we encounter people and cope with people, so we do in our dreams. Only that is the beauty of the dream—the dream fulfills many more functions than just this—but we can start with the fact that we encounter the people who are the things in the dreams and that every bit of the dream, every other person, every thing, every mood is part of our fractionalized self. Now this is so important that I would like to reformulate it again. We are as we are today—fractionalized people—people who are split up into bits and pieces. And it's no use to analyze these bits and pieces and cut them up still more. What we want to do in Gestalt therapy is to integrate all the dispersed and disowned alienated parts of the self and make the person whole again. A wholesome person is a person who functions well, can rely on his own resources, and can resume his growth, wherever the person gets stuck in his growth.

So what I would like to do is again to start on the basis of dream work, and I have to say this: When you meet another person, and this person feels the need to tell you a dream, then this person will tell you the dream as a story. Now this is the first step—the story. The second step is to revive the dream and we do this by making just a grammatical change. Instead of telling a story, we tell a drama. And we do it simply by changing the past tense into the present tense. I am climbing a mountain. There comes this and this and this. The third step is we play the stage director, we set the stage. Here's the mountain. Here am I. You notice, slowly we are getting a live performance of the dream. And often we recover quite a bit of the vividness of the dream. We begin to realize we are the author, we are the stage director. So then we can go into the next step and do more. We become not only the author and stage director, we become also the actor and the props and everything that is there. And then we see there are plenty of encounters possible. Plenty of opportunities for two things: One is to integrate conflicts and the other is to re-identify with the alienated parts. If we have alienated parts of ourselves—if we are disowned—we re-own them by re-identifying, by becoming those parts again. We have to become the villain and the demon, and realize that those are all projected parts of ourselves.

So we encounter for the first time the idea of projection. Projection is the disowning of a part of ourself which then appears in the outer world, our personal world, and ceases to be a part of ourselves. Now, the re-owning of many of these parts is unpleasant. We don't like to realize that we are a sewer or a policeman. This is where the moment of learning to suffer comes in. To suffer from the moment of the idea that we might be a sewer or a policeman—and then suddenly it appears that there are valuable energies somewhere hidden in those projections. We can assimilate these and make them our own again. There are many more things to the dream which I don't want to mention right now. But the one thing is this: You don't have to work for the whole dream. Even if you only take a dream and re-identify with a few of the items, each time you assimilate one item you grow—you increase your potential. You begin to change.

So, let's work first a little bit on such little bits and samples. Let's go through the four stages with a few of you just to get the idea across that we can do this systematically, and something will happen. Who wants to volunteer?

Russ: I was on this mountain, kind of like the hills back of here, and there was a friend of mine, a close friend, and he was sitting on his knees. And he seemed okay. And he had a pot, and a blue plate, and some kind of bowl, just kind of arranged in a row.

Fritz: Good. Now take the second step. Tell the whole section of the dream—I guess that's not the whole dream—get the whole, the same section again, in the present tense.

Russ: Chris is sitting—you're sitting right in front of me. On your knees. And right in front of you I see a pot and a blue plate and a bowl. (To Fritz) Shall I go on with the rest of it?

Fritz: No. I just want to take sections to get you to set the stage. Make a play out of this. Here's your stage. Where does he sit, where is the plate, and so on.

Russ: Chris, here's Chris, here's the pot, the plate, and this bowl, and then in the background the mountains, and then there's kind of straw, dried grass, around. I'm right here, looking. I was walking up this trail which continues around the back of the mountains. And then I just stop.

Fritz: Can you do this once more? I think you're a bit lazy. Get up, and really set the stage, show us the whole drama.

Russ: The trail—it's coming up here and it continues . . .

Fritz: Where, where?

Russ: Pardon?

Fritz: Continue around the hill.

Russ: See you later, Chris.

Fritz: Okay.

Russ: There he is again. (Walks in a circle, stops in front of the hot seat)

Fritz: Don't look at me, now. You produce, and you talk to the different actors. You're now the producer.

Russ: (Shrugs) Well, what's happening? What are these? The pot, the plate, and the bowl. What are you doing? (Switches to be Chris) Watch this. (He takes the plates and starts shooting around like a nut in a shell game, demonstrating with a sweeping motion of his hands) Watch this. Now, what do you think is under this pot?

The blue plate. What do you think is under this blue plate? The pot.

Fritz: Okay. Now you become all the different actors. You become your friend, you become the plate, you become the trail. And if you have difficulty, you start saying this. If I would be a trail, I would have this and this kind of existence. Let me warn you, there's only one great mistake you can make. That is to interpret. If you start interpreting, you're lost. You make an intellectual, Freudian game out of it, and at best, you will be filing away some very interesting insights into some intellectual filing cabinet, and make sure nothing real happens. Don't interpret, just be that thing, be that plate, be that pot, be that friend of yours.

Russ: Chris, watch this Russ. See what I can do. See if you can keep up with me. It's kind of catchy.

Fritz: Now for instance, if we would already be working on him, I would tell him now, turn around . . .

Russ: You mean, now?

Fritz: Turn around. Be the same guy, and play this to the audience.

Russ: (To group) Watch this. See if you can keep up with it. It's pretty damn fast. Now, what do you think's under this pot? The plate, right? Okay, now what do you think is under the plate? The pot. What do you think is under the pot? The plate—all at the same time.

Fritz: Now, you notice how different he behaves from the timid guy yesterday? Do you feel comfortable in that role right now?

Russ: I feel comfortable and evasive as all hell.

Fritz: Good. So be the different other thing. Be the trail.

Russ: Okay. (Pause) I am a trail.

Fritz: What is your purpose, Trail? What is your shape and condition?

Russ: I'm a trail. I'm on this mountain. I'm a nice

trail. It's comfortable. I'm not too hard to walk on.

Fritz: Say this again.

Russ: I'm not too hard to walk on. (Pause) There's a lot of nice scenery along me. Nice places to go, a few campsites. I, uh, go up to the top of the mountain. People walk on me to the top.

Fritz: Say this again.

Russ: People walk on me up to the top. (Pause) That hurt.

Fritz: See. You didn't interpret. Something came through.

Russ: Russ is walking on me, but he stopped. He's with Chris now. He's still on me.

Fritz: Good. Now we have here a definite encounter which we can use. Sit down here. We interrupt the dream now for some encounter bit. You are the trail and there's Russ. (Points to the empty chair) And you both talk to each other. Write the script.

Russ: You're walking on me, I know. You're not too bad. Your boots are kind of heavy, more than most. (Switches to Chris) Well, I think they have to be to assure good traction, you know. (Russ) You wear me down. I, you, you've been walking on me an awful lot, fellow, with heavy boots. Why don't you get off me? Why do you need a fucking trail? Shit, you don't need me. You got your big boots, go do your own thing. (Chris) If I get off you, Trail, I might get lost. I might fall down. You're safe. You're even—it's all been arranged. Somebody else has gone there and like I say, I can't get lost.

Fritz: All right, I want to interrupt here. You notice that something is beginning to happen already. You feel that you're being stirred up.

Russ. Yeah.

Fritz: We just approach a little bit of a segment of a dream, do a little bit of work. Actually, I believe if one takes a dream and completes its work, that's all the therapy that is required.

Only what usually happens is that once you are developing a little more of your personality, another dream will come up which sends you another existential message. This, for me, is the meaning of the dream—an existential message. It's not just an unfinished situation, it's not just a current problem, it's not just a symptom or character formation. It's an existential meaning, a message. It concerns your total existence, concerns your total lifescript. Okay, let's have somebody else. (Ann goes to the hot seat) Your name is?

Ann: Ann. This is a dream that I have frequently, with slightly varying detail, and it's not . . .

Fritz: We interrupt again. These are the most important dreams and here I take a completely different stand from Freud. Freud saw the compulsive repetition—having to repeat something over and over—and he concluded that this was the function of the death instinct. I believe these repetitive dreams are an attempt to come to a solution, to come to a closure. We have to get the obstacle out of the way so that the person can finish the situation, close the gestalt and then go on to further development. And you can be sure if there is a repetitive dream, it's a very important existential issue at stake.

Ann: I'm traveling on a train, with a group. We're all going somewhere—I don't know where. But we stop at a station and I leave the group. My husband is usually a part of the group, and I leave him as well. He's going somewhere else. I go off in another train by myself. And soon I realize that I've forgotten where my destination is. When I try and locate myself I realize I don't remember where I've been so I can't locate myself from looking backwards either.

Fritz: Okay, let's start with the beginning. You already skipped the first step, you told the story in the present tense. So now, set the stage.

Ann: I'm traveling on a train with a loosely knit group. I don't really know . . . I don't feel, uh, these people as being friends or enemies or strangers or any particular thing. We're all just going along together, and sitting somehow, in this group. We're sort of jogging along as the train moves. (Pauses and rocks in a jogging motion) I don't feel that we're really communicating or that we're going anywhere in particular. Just moving. We get to this station and the group seems to disperse somewhat. We get off the train.

Fritz: Now can you be the director and tell them each exactly what they should do? I notice you were sitting again on your butt, and not getting off the train and not starting to communicate.

Ann: Okay. We get off the train now. And we come into a very big station with big pillars—one of these big old grey stone stations with huge pillars. And we don't really go inside to any room. We stand sort of out in the big foyer with these pillars. And I'm standing pretty close to this pillar and I'm not talking to anybody. I feel the other group is around here but we're not, uh, really not connected.

Fritz: All right. May I suggest that you pick out the pillar? Play the pillar and play the station. If you were a pillar, what kind of existence would you lead?

Ann: Being a pillar in this huge old railway station, I see a lot of people come and go here. Some of them seem to know where they're going and some of them stay quite close to me for support. (Starts to cry)

Fritz: Something begins to happen. Now be the station.

Ann: I'm a big old solid railway station. A lot of people come through me . . . and I give some comfort. And sort of a place for people when they're sort of, when they stop or when they're going somewhere. If people want to come inside I have food for them, and restrooms and a place to sit and, and be comfortable.

Fritz: Okay, let's use this for an encounter. Sit

down here. You're Ann and this is the station. You both talk to each other. I guess you already noticed how much of the personality is being expressed by the different essences. I don't call them symbols, they're essences of the personality.

Ann: I have come to you, station, on the train and stopped here with the group, but I haven't come inside (wipes her eyes) where I might find some comfort (crying) or someone who would look after me. (Station) Why didn't you want to? Why didn't you want to stop and sit and have something to eat and sort of rest a while before you went on? That's what stations are for. (Ann) I'm a little afraid of sort of stopping and being comfortable. I feel I have to keep moving even if I don't know where I'm going. (Station) Why do you . . . it doesn't make any sense that you keep moving on, getting on another train and going off somewhere and you don't even know where you've been and where you're going or . . . you have friends here and you leave them behind.

Fritz: Well, this sounds already like a little bit of an existential message. Okay, this is as far as I want to go.

Madeline's Dream

When I first broke away from Freud and psychoanalysis, I wrote a book called *Ego Hunger and Aggression,* and I produced, I would say, three basic new theories—the awareness theory, the theory of the I, and the theory of aggression. Now you know that the awareness theory is widely accepted under all kinds of names—encounter groups, expanding of consciousness, and so on. The whole awareness kick is becoming a fad in the United States. For instance, a little bit of aggression is accepted as being not a bad thing, but a biological function of the organism. Especially of the teeth and assimilation. Aggression is too often equated with hostility and so on. Again, I don't want to go into the details of this theory—I just want to mention that this aggression is required to assimilate the world. If we don't assimilate what is available, we can't make it our own part of ourselves. It remains a foreign body in our system—something which Freud recognized as introjection. And this leads us to the ego theory. Freud saw the ego, which in German is the same as 'I,' as a conglomeration of foreign substances which, if it's true, would always remain a conglomeration of foreign bodies in our organism. Now here again is where the merit of the Gestalt approach comes in. A gestalt is always differentiated between foreground and background, and the foreground relation to the background is called 'meaning.' In other words, according to my idea, as soon as you tear something out of its context, it loses its meaning or distorts its meaning. Now this figure background relationship applies very much to the I. The I is an identification symbol. Let me compare the two contexts.

The whole semantic approach is completely cockeyed. There are only two semantic approaches known. One is the so-called absolute approach—a thing means what it is, or as it is defined by the dictionary or whatever. The meaning of a tree is just as it's being described, as the so-called absolute semantic. The other is the Alice in Wonderland semantic. A thing means what I mean it to mean. The Gestalt approach is different. It says a meaning is a creation at this moment of the relationship of the foreground figure to its background. In other words, as soon as you tear something out of its context, it loses its meaning or distorts its meaning. Take the idea of a queen. In the context of a chess game it is a piece of carved wood. In the context of the British Empire, it is a living person that is supposed to rule millions of people. Now if the absolute semantic would be correct, you could take this piece of chess board and put it on the throne of England or we could take Queen Elizabeth and put her on the chess board. It would look a bit funny, wouldn't it?

Now see how this leads up to our whole neurosis

treatment. In a neurosis, the parts of the personality are all alienated. If you identify with these alienated parts, we can now get ready to assimilate disowned parts and grow again—become more whole. It's very interesting that, for instance, some primitive tribes who do not differentiate between the self and the world, don't have the word "I." They say "here." Here's light, here's hunger, here's anger, here's thought, here's a deer. And a child also has quite a difficulty in understanding the word I. He says, "Carl is hungry." He still calls himself by the name that is given to him.

Now I would like to integrate more the idea of dream work and total identification work. So, who wants to work on a dream? (Madeline comes forward—a pretty dark-haired French girl.) This time, as much as possible, I want you to always return to your experience. Right now—what do you feel right now?

Madeline: Um . . .

Fritz: You feel 'um.' Keep your eyes and ears open. Every clue is to be accepted.

Madeline: I feel like taking my shoes off. (Laughs) I feel the need to be clear when I tell my dream.

Fritz: Okay.

Madeline: Uh, the dream I have, I experienced when I was very young, maybe about eight years old, and I've experienced it even lately. I'm standing on the shore. The shore is sort of sandy and soft and there's wood around me. In front, there's a lake that is very round. I don't see the other end of the lake where I'm standing right now, but the lake, I know, is very round, or I find it out later. But I feel it is very round, very circular, and not edgy shore. It's a very soft lake and the light is very beautiful. There is not sun, but it is very bright in the sky.

Fritz: Ya. Let me work on the dream a bit. Be the lake. And Lake, tell me your story.

Madeline: Um, lake, uh, you want to tell me your story?

Fritz: Be a lake and tell me your story.

Madeline: Uh, I'm a round, round lake. I feel, I sort

of feel perfect, perfect lake. I, my water is very good and soft to the touch.

Fritz: To whom are you talking?

Madeline: To myself.

Fritz: Now you know the third law in Gestalt therapy. Do unto others what you do unto yourself. Talk to us.

Madeline: Um . . .

Fritz: You're the lake.

Madeline: I'm the lake. You would like to come in me, in my lake, in this lake, because it's very beautiful, and the water feels very . . .

Fritz: The second law in Gestalt therapy—don't say it; say I or you.

Madeline: Um . . . (moves a little)

Fritz: You notice I'm beginning to become very officious.

Madeline: You would like to come into me. You can swim into me very easily and there's nothing mucky in my bottom. My bottom is of pure sand. And when you come into the middle of my lake, there's a surprise. There's something that you don't know. And it might frighten you or you might like it very much, but there's something right in the middle of me, in the lake, that is very strange, and you have to swim or row to get to it. You don't see it from the shore, so it's really worth swimming to go and see it. (Laughs)

Fritz: See 'it'?

Madeline: See me. (Laughs)

Fritz: Say this again to the group.

Madeline: It's worth swimming in me or taking a boat, not a power boat.

Fritz: Who is 'it'? 'Its' worth.

Madeline: Uh, its worth to you?

Fritz: Who is 'it,' 'it' is worth?

Madeline: The . . . it is worth . . .

Fritz: Don't say 'it.' Try 'I'. 'I' am worth.

Madeline: I am. I am worth—you swimming or taking a boat and coming to see what's in the middle of the lake, because it's a surprise.

Fritz: 'It' is a surprise?

Madeline: Uh, I am a surprise. You might not solve the surprise, though. It's a, I have in . . . the middle of my lake, I have a statue. It's a little boy, and he's pouring water . . . but many people . . . when I go in that lake and I come to drink the water, I wake up, so maybe . . .

Fritz: Wait, stop here. Close your eyes. Go on dreaming. Now the waking up is a beautiful gimmick to interrupt the solution to the dream.

Madeline: The . . .

Fritz: You came back to us. Did you go on dreaming?

Madeline: The same dream? It took a long time before I came to the dream. I saw the lights in my eyes and feeling of, of very busy.

Fritz: Gesticulate this. Go on.

Madeline: Very busy. (Moves arms about and laughs)

Fritz: Dance it. (She does a dance mostly with arm movements.) All right. Now let's have the story of the figure of the statue. You're now the statue.

Madeline: I'm a statue in the middle of the lake.

Fritz: To whom are you talking?

Madeline: I was trying to talk to Helen. (Laughs) I'm grey and sort of, uh, I'm pretty classical looking. I'm looking like most little statues of little boys you would see. And I hold a vessel. It is a vase that has a small neck and big in the bottom. And I hold it, and though I'm in the water, I pour it—I pour this water in the lake. I don't know where it comes from, but this water is extremely pure, and you would really benefit from drinking this water. You would feel all good all over because you had water on the outside of your body from the lake I am sitting in the middle of. And the water is really good outside of your body. But then, I really want you to drink the water I'm giving from my vessel because it will really make you feel good inside, also. I don't know why, but sometimes, you cannot drink it, you just come to drink it—you're all happy and then you're swimming and you want to drink it and then you can't drink it. I cannot bend to you. I can just keep on pouring my water and then hoping you can come and drink it.

Fritz: Say that last sentence again to us.

Madeline: I cannot come down and give the water to you. I just can keep on pouring it and hoping that you will come and drink it. I just can keep on pouring it.

Fritz: Okay. Now, play the water. Tell us. You're now the water.

Madeline: In the vessel?

Fritz: Yes, the water in the vessel. What's your script? What's your story, Water?

Madeline: (Pause) I don't know much about myself.

Fritz: And again.

Madeline: I don't know much about myself. (Pause, begins to cry) I come. I don't know how I come but I know I'm good, that's all I know. I would like you to drink me because I know I'm good. I don't know where I come from . . . I'm in that big vase. It's a black vase.

Fritz: Now, get up. Say this to each one of us. Stand up. Go to each one of us and tell us this. You're the water.

Madeline: (Crying and sniffing) I'm water in a vase and I don't know where I come from. But I know I'm good to drink. I'm water in a vase.

Fritz: Use your own words now.

Madeline: I look like water and they call me water and I'm just there in the vase. And there's no hole in the vase. I don't know where, nobody, I'm just there all the time, I'm just pouring out, and I'd like you to drink me.

Fritz: Go on to the next.

Madeline: I'm there and I'm white and pure, and if you ask me where I come from I can't tell you. But it's a miracle, I always come out, just for you to drink me. You have to get out of the other water and come. (Goes to the next person, crying) I'm in a vase, and I don't know where

I come from but I'm coming out all the time, and you have to drink me, every little bit of it.

Fritz: Now what are you doing with yourself?

Madeline: I'm holding myself.

Fritz: Do this to me. (Goes over to him and rubs his arms) Okay, sit down. So what do you experience now?

Madeline: I feel I've discovered something.

Fritz: Yeah? What?

Madeline: I used to think, I thought of the dreams, I used to think the water in the vase was spirituality.

Fritz: Mmhhmm.

Madeline: Beauty of, of birth and . . . it's such a mystery for me, the beauty of life, and I thought that the vase was a secret, and I wasn't high enough to drink the water. That's why I woke up. When I was very small, it didn't bother me —I was just happy of swimming. I didn't care not drinking the water, waking up. But as I grew older I got more and more resentful not to be able to drink the water . . .

Fritz: All right. This is as far as I want to go. Again, you see the same thing that we did before with dreams. No interpretation. You know everything; you know much more than I do and all my interpretations would only mislead you. It's again, simply the question of learning, of uncovering your true self.

Everything is Aware Process

Well, the time has come that we might be ready to put all the pieces together and see whether we can get a center of approach. And the basic center is, of course, to unify the whole world into one. You can do it with the help of religion—by saying everything is God made. But then you still are left with the dichotomy between God and the world, and the doubt whether the world has made God or God the world. If, however, we consider the three dimensions possible—extension, duration, and awareness—then we can say everything is an aware process. We are still very reluctant to attribute awareness to matter, we are so used to believing that awareness is concentrated in the brain. It's very difficult in the beginning to imagine that the whole world—and we're getting more and more scientific proof—always has awareness.

So, everything is an aware process. Let's start from there. I am aware. You are aware. The chair is aware of me—maybe in a fraction of a billionth and billionth of a unit of awareness. But I'm sure that awareness is there. As soon as we accept this, another dichotomy begins to collapse between the objective and the subjective. The subjective is always awareness and the objective is the content of awareness. We have to be aware that we are not aware of anything. Without awareness there is nothing. So there is a contrast between the existent and the non-existent or the nothingness. Awareness is always linked up with the present experience. We cannot possibly be aware of the past and cannot possibly be aware of the future. We are aware of memories, we are aware of anticipation, and of plans of the future; but we are aware here and now—a part of the aware process.

The decisive awareness is the awareness of the uniqueness of each one of us. We experience ourselves as a unique something, whether we like to call it personality or soul or essence. And we are also aware that we are all the time aware of something different, that we are in a different place at a different time. So we try always to get hold and find out—and always start in Gestalt therapy with the idea: where are you? Where are you in time; where are you in place? Are you all there or are you at home attending to some unfinished business, and where are you in your awareness? Are you in touch with the world, are you in touch with yourself, are you in touch with the middle zone—the fantasy life that is interfering with being completely in touch with yourself or the world?

When we are in touch with the world, then something happens. What makes us get in touch with the world is the emerging Gestalt, the emerging need, and the emerging unfinished situation. And if we cannot cope with that situation, we look for support—something, somebody to help us to cope. And that support can be secured by manipulating the environment, by crying for help, by playing helpless, playing crybaby, or controlling the world. Or we get the support from within ourselves—we withdraw into ourselves to find this support. And we always find something when we withdraw. We might find the support from the self, or we might only find the support from our fantasy life. That support has to be thoroughly examined because that support might be a catastrophic expectation. That support might say—don't cope; if you cope it might be dangerous. Or the support will say—oh yes, grab it, it will be heaven.

A world of fools. But in each case, in this shuttle between coping and looking for support for coping, we start to mobilize our own potential. This, I would say, is the whole theory and approach in a nutshell. And as I said before, there's no better means to get to understand the middle zone, the disturbing factor, than the dream. So we always work around the dream and other non-verbal ways of being to empty out, brainwash, whatever you want to call it, that cancer or sick part of the personality. So who's got a dream they want to work on? (Helen goes to the hot seat. She is a bright, plump woman around forty.)

Helen: We're sitting around in an encounter group and everybody is in a director's chair. The room changes back and forth between two rooms that I'm familiar with—Maslow and your living room. The way I know we change back and forth is that the rug changes from a thin, sort of red and black dusty rug, to a thick deep-piled rug . . .

Fritz: Okay, let's have these two rugs have an encounter.

Helen: (Smiles) I'm the thick, juicy, orange, deep piled, soft rich rug. And, uh, if you sit on me, I bend very nicely. And I like my warm, orangey color.

And I'm a kind of thin, red and black, dusty, arid, smelly rug. And everything that touches me hurts me because I'm so thin. And I'm neglected . . . I feel alone, and as if nobody really cared to clean me or anything.

Fritz: You're telling me this. What about telling it to the other rug?

Helen: I envy you. I really envy you. Because people like to sit on you, and when they sit on me, they feel their bones. I wish they'd at least put a pad under me.

(Smiling) I don't blame you for envying me. I am very nice and soft. Sometimes people cry on me, but you can't see their tears because I just soak them all up. And even stains don't show very much on me, and I don't have anything left over to feel very sorry for you. Because I'm so busy enjoying myself, and I don't really like to look at you because you're dilapidated. And I'm just so happy to be me! (Laughs) Well, I feel a little bad about you.

Fritz: All right, let's do the same with the opposition of the Maslow room and my living room. Let these two rooms meet each other.

Helen: I'm all made of wood, and I have lovely grains on my wall, and my rug is deep and thick. I have big windows that have lovely wooden carvings that partially cover the view from the outside in, but make the view from inside out even better than it would be without the shades. My main problem is that the lighting is lousy. Half the time the lighting is wrong and the heat is wrong.

I'm a cluttered, austere, stony, thin-rugged room with an unused fireplace, and a view I can't see, and so crowded and cluttered, and unsupportive. But I have something you don't have. I have the sound of the ocean very close, and it fills the room most of the time. And my heating system is pretty good and I've got lots of outlets and plugs.

Fritz: You sound defensive and disappointed.

Helen: Yes, I am. And I feel a little sad. Because I'm Fritz Perls' living room and there's no life in me, except the sound of the sea. I'm aware of my dust and hardness and the clutteredness.

(Smiling) I'm the room of dozens of people and I do feel warm. And another thing, I don't like to look at you very much, because I feel I've got so much more than you've got and when I look at you I'm aware of what's lacking.

Fritz: Say this again.

Helen: I really don't want to look at you.

Fritz: Again.

Helen: I really don't want to look at you.

Fritz: Louder.

Helen: I really don't want to look at you!

Fritz: Say it with your whole body.

Helen: I don't want to look at you!

Fritz: Now change seats.

Helen: For Christ's sake, I didn't say you had to look at me! Don't look at me if you don't want to! But don't shout at me! (Shouting) I hate to be shouted at! I'm angry! (Pause) So you got what you wanted. I don't have what I want. I don't have what I need.

Fritz: Say this again.

Helen: I don't have what I need. (Pause, continues quietly) And I don't know how to get it. There are structural limitations in stone and cement and thinness. (Pause) I forgot to breathe for a minute. (Takes a deep breath)

Fritz: Can you close your eyes and enter your body and see what you experience physically?

Helen: My cheeks are hot and my voice is hoarse. My throat is tight. There's a sadness at the back of my throat and down in my chest. And I'm breathing rather deeply, and it feels good. It comforts and reassures me. I'm wetting my lips because they feel dry. I'm aware of how I'm sitting—it's as if I was about to take off. I'm also highly defensive and covered. My right shoulder is way forward and my right hand is poised as if I were ready to do something.

Fritz: To do what?
Helen: Slap.
Fritz: So slap the Maslow room. (She does so a few times.) Now do it with your left hand, too.
Helen: I don't want to slap it with my left hand. (Smiles) I want to touch it. (Reaches out)
Fritz: All right, can you do this alternately now? Slap with your right hand and touch with your left. (She does this about three times.) Now do me a favor, even if it's phony. Exchange hands. Slap with your left hand and touch with your right.
Helen: Mmhhmm. I can touch with my right.
Fritz: What do you experience then?
Helen: It's nice, I like it. I can feel just as much with my right hand as I can with my left. I feel very reluctant to hit with my left.
Fritz: Say this to the Maslow room.
Helen: I don't want to hit you with my left hand. I really only want to touch you. I don't want to hit you.
Fritz: Try once more.
Helen: To hit?
Fritz: Ya. With your left hand.
Helen: I'm amazed at my reluctance. I really don't want to.
Fritz: Say this again.
Helen: I really don't want to.
Fritz: Again.
Helen: I don't want to hit you!
Fritz: And again.
Helen: I don't want to hit you. (Smiling, voice changes to a more tender, teasing tone) I don't want to hit you. (Laughter) I don't want to hit you. I just want to touch you.
Fritz: Now, try once more to hit.
Helen: I can do it, but my heart won't be in it.
Fritz: Well, try it.
Helen: (Laughs) Didn't hurt. (Touches with both hands) Feels much nicer to feel with both hands.
Fritz: Well, hit again with your left hand. You

see, I find something irrational here, so I'm going to work on that.

Helen: If I look at you I can hit you. (Hits chair, then kicks it very methodically) Yeah, if I look at you, I can hit you and I can kick you. I can really hate you. (Pause) You're shiny. I envy you. No, I don't envy you, goddammit, you've got your thing. You're just different. (Quieter) I envy you.

Fritz: Change seats.

Helen: Hi. I don't like it when you hit me. I know I've got a lot that you don't have, but I just arrived that way. It isn't anything that I've grabbed for myself from something else. From somebody else, from you. I happened just the way you happened but I didn't take anything from you.

One part of me wants to plead with you and one part of me wants to shove you away. I wish you weren't just so lush. A little moderation in lush. It's this fulsomeness that I can't stand.

Fritz: Say this again with your left hand.

Helen: It's this fulsomeness that I can't stand. (To Fritz) It doesn't feel right. (Pause) It's this, I envy your fulsomeness. (Smiles) I feel rueful about it. Kind of, as if I wanted something I really can't have and I don't want to be content with what I've got.

Fritz: Say this to the group.

Helen: I don't want to be content with what I've got.

Fritz: Can you elaborate on this?

Helen: Yeah, I've got a lot, but I've had a glimpse of so much more. And so I want it. And I'm willing to work very hard and spend a lot of time and effort to get more. And what I've had a glimpse of is more of me. And I'm really excited about me and I'd like to have more of me; but that involves working with other people and there I get scared. Real scared (smiles at Fritz) in some places, not in others.

Fritz: Okay, that's how far I want to go. I guess you noticed something I did. I did very little directing. But when I feel and notice there is some irrationality involved, then I work on that place until the whole issue becomes rational again. And this is something for which you really need to develop a tremendous amount of sensitivity and intuition. This is the key sentence. If one feels there is a key sentence involved—something really basic—then I reinforce it, let her talk again, speak over again and reinforce it till the whole personality comes through. Then you notice something completely unexpected happens. The personality gets involved, and the emotions, and there is again a turning point in the growth process.

Fritz, Friend, and Freud

(Barbara is seated in the hot seat. She is a young woman who appears to be about 38 years old, with a rather diffident manner. She is a social worker, and has worked with Fritz before.)

Barbara: I wanted to be a good girl and have a magnificent dream for you with lots of goodies in it. I didn't manage that, but something else happened which is maybe just as well. Last night I was in bed, and it's happened to me for a long time—though not very frequently—and what happens is I become totally paralyzed and I can't move at all. I can't move my toes and I can't open my eyes—I can't do anything. I'm just totally paralyzed. And I get very frightened and then it goes away. It seems like a very long time, but I think it's just a few minutes—maybe not even that long. But it's like I can't do anything, and what it made me think of was, uh, my inability to handle myself when I get frightened or angry. (Takes a long drag on her cigarette) I just get immobilized—so that I'm the same when I'm awake as when asleep, I'm still paralyzed.

Fritz: All right. Could you tell the whole story again and imagine that you are responsible for all that happens. For instance, "I paralyze myself."

Barbara: Um, all right. Um, I paralyze, I paralyze myself . . . I immobilize myself. I won't allow myself to feel anything or behave any way if it isn't civilized and good. I won't let myself run away when I'm afraid; I won't tell people I'm afraid. I won't, uh, fight back when I'm angry or hurt. I won't ever let people know that I have bad feelings. (Starts to cry) I won't let them know that I hate them sometimes, or that I'm scared to death and, um . . . I put myself sometimes, to punish myself, in a state of panic where I'm scared to do anything. I'm scared to breathe, and then I torture myself with all the bad things I'll let happen to me. That's all I can think of right now. (Sniffs) Fritz, I don't want to cry because I think that crying is very bad for me. I think I hide behind my tears. But I don't know what I . . . hide.

(Barbara is slapping her thigh with her hand as she talks.)

Fritz: Can you do this again? With your right hand. Talk to Barbara.

Barbara: (Slapping her thigh and laughing) Barbara, you need a spanking!

Fritz: Spank her.

Barbara: (Still slapping) You're a bad girl because you're phony and dishonest! You lie to yourself and to everybody else, and I'm tired of it because it doesn't work!

Fritz: What does Barbara answer?

Barbara: (Voice rising) She answers that she never learned how to do anything else.

Fritz: Say this in quotes.

Barbara: I never learned how to do anything else. I know about doing other things. I know that there are other things to do but I don't know how to do them.

Fritz: Say this again.

Barbara: I don't know how to do them! I can only do them when I'm in a protected, supporting kind of situation; then I can do it a little bit. But if I'm out in a cold situation by myself I'm too scared. And then I get into trouble. I get myself into trouble.

Fritz: Ya.

Barbara: And then I get mad at myself after I've gotten myself into trouble, and then I punish and punish and punish. (Spanks thigh again) And it's like there is no end to it, and I'll never be satisfied. (Starts to cry)

Fritz: Say this to Barbara. I'll never be satisfied with you, whatever you do I'm never satisfied.

Barbara: Barbara, I'm never satisfied with you. No matter what you do it's never good enough!

Fritz: Can you say this to your mother or father as well?

Barbara: Mother, no matter what I do or have done, it's never been good enough.

Fritz: Can you also say this to her? Mother, whatever you do it's never good enough.

Barbara: Uh huh. Mother, whatever you do, it isn't good enough.

Fritz: Tell her what she should do.

Barbara: Mother, you should try to know me. You don't know me. I'm a stranger, and you let me pretend . . . you know, and I have a whole personality just for you. And that's not me. I'm not at all the kind of person that you think I am.

Fritz: What would she answer?

Barbara: Of course I understand you, you're my daughter. I understand everything about you. And I know what's good for you!

Fritz: Talk back.

Barbara: Mother, you don't know what's good for me! Your ways don't work for me. I don't like them and I don't respect your attitudes. I just don't think they're productive. I think that they leave you alone, and you never get close to people. You always disapprove of them too much. You don't like anybody, and I don't want to be that kind of person . . .

Fritz: Tell her more what she should do. What kind of person she should be.

Barbara: You should try to understand how it is for other people. They experience life very differently from you. Couldn't you just try once to know what it is to be somebody else?

Fritz: Ya. I would like you to go a step further. Talk to her in the form of an imperative. "Be more understanding" and so on.

Barbara: Be more understanding . . .

Fritz: All imperatives.

Barbara: Be more empathetic! Be more sensitive! Don't defend yourself so much, you don't need to! Don't be so suspicious and paranoid! Don't believe in magic, it's crazy to believe in magic! Don't always be in a double bind, where you're trying to be such a good person, such a saintly person, such a paragon of the community, such a matriarch, and hating every minute of it. Don't do that!

Fritz: Now, talk like this to Barbara. Also in imperatives.

Barbara: Barbara, don't be helpless! That's crazy . . . uh . . . don't be afraid of your feelings! Your bad feelings—you have to express them. You've got to stand up for yourself! You've got to be real! Don't play hide and seek, that's a rotten game! (Starts to cry) Don't be a mess, and don't play games where other people feel sorry for you or feel guilty. Then they'll get uncomfortable and go away and that isn't what you want.

Fritz: Now go into more detail. Stick to your imperatives, and each time give Barbara some prescription—what she should do to follow up.

Barbara: Um . . . don't be a mime, a chameleon!

Fritz: Tell her how she should achieve this—not to be a chameleon.

Barbara: Figure out who you are, and what you want to be and what to do, and do it! Don't try to go around looking for other people to imitate all the time. You've imitated thousands of people and where has it ever gotten you? You still feel like an empty shell. You've got to decide who you are, and what you want to do!

Fritz: Tell her how she can decide.

Barbara: (In a scolding tone) You know what your own tastes and interests and values are. You've known for a long time. They're never . . .

Fritz: Tell her in detail what her interests are.

Barbara: Um, lots of things interest you.

Fritz: Such as?

Barbara: Such as . . . you like to work with people and it makes you feel very good when you feel that you've been useful—that you've allowed yourself to be used in a productive kind of way by other people. Do that! And figure out a way to do it in which you feel successful and useful.

Fritz: Come on, start figuring out.

Barbara: Well, you have to develop . . . you have to do two things: You have to make a real effort to learn from other people who are much more experienced and skilled than you are and at the same time you've got to be yourself. You can't go around imitating Fritz or Virginia Satir or Dr. Delchamps or whoever the consultant of the moment is, or wherever the last seminar you went to was or the last workshop. Don't do that, that's bad! Because you're not them and you can't just go through the motions that they go through, and say things they say, and do any good for anybody. They'll know that you're a phony.

Fritz: You mentioned my name. So, tell me, what am I? What are you copying of me?

Barbara: Fritz, you're a man who works with people and lets them use him—you let people use you to grow.

Fritz: Ya.

Barbara: And I want to do that too, and I think that what you do really works . . . but I can't play Fritz. That won't work because I'm not you and my tendency would be to imitate you.

Fritz: Let me see how you imitate me. You play Fritz.

Barbara: (Laughs) All right. Shall I do it with you?

Fritz: Ya.

Barbara: All right. (Laughing)
(Long pause) Do you want to work?

Fritz: Yes.

Barbara: Do you not want me to work? For you?

Fritz: Yes.

Barbara: I can't, Fritz. I can't work for you.

Fritz: Oh yes you can.

Barbara: No.

Fritz: (With a gleam in his eye) You're Fritz, you know everything. (Laughter) You're so wise.

Barbara: It's not true. I don't know everything, and I'm not that wise. You have to do the work.

Fritz: All right. I try so hard. I would like to work, but I can't. I have got a block. (General hilarity at Fritz's responses)

Barbara: Be your block.

Fritz: But I can't see my block.

Barbara: You're not listening to me.

Fritz: Oh yes, I'm listening very carefully. I just heard you say, "You're not listening to me."

Barbara: Well, let's see if we can try something else. Pretend you're out there.

Fritz: Out there?

Barbara: Uh huh.

Fritz: Where? Here, or there, or there, or there? (Pointing to different places in the room)

Barbara: Wherever you choose.

Fritz: You choose for me.

Barbara: I feel like you're making fun of me. And maybe trying . . .

Fritz: Me? Making fun of you? I wouldn't dare! You're so venerable and I just melt with appreciation. I wouldn't dare to make fun of you. How could I?

Barbara: Let's try something else then. Can you dance your veneration of me?

Fritz: Oh yes. (Laughter) Now I can't do a thing. You have to give me the music.

Barbara: Uh, try making up the music in your own head.

Fritz: But I'm not musical, you see.

Barbara: We're all musical.

Fritz: You do it. (Laughter)

Barbara: I notice that no matter what happens, the burden returns to me. No matter what I suggest, you say no, you do it for me, I don't know how.

Fritz: Of course. If I weren't so incapable, I wouldn't be here. This is my illness, don't you see?

Barbara: Talk to your illness.

Fritz: But my illness isn't here. How can I talk to my illness? And if I could talk to the illness, the illness wouldn't listen, because this is the illness.

Barbara: I'll listen. Did someone give you the illness?

Fritz: (Slowly) Yes.

Barbara: Who?

Fritz: Sigmund Freud. (There is much laughing among the group at this point.)

Barbara: I realize that Sigmund isn't here, that he's . . .

Fritz: But for seven years I got infected.

Barbara: (Giggling) Oh, I'm three years above you because I spent ten years with an analyst. Don't tell me how bad it is! Could you talk to Sigmund?

Fritz: Oh no, I can't. He's dead.

Barbara: You've changed. That's the first time you've slipped. What are you aware of now?

Fritz: (Soberly) A great sorrow that Freud is dead

before I really could talk as man to man with him.

Barbara: (Gently) I think you could still talk to him. Would you like to?

Fritz: Uh huh.

Barbara: Fine. (Pause) I'd like to listen.

Fritz: Now I'm stuck. I would like to do it. I would like to be your patient in this situation, and uh . . . (speaking very slowly) Professor Freud . . . a great man . . . but very sick . . . you can't let anyone touch you. You've got to say what is and your word is holy gospel. I wish you would listen to me. In a certain way I know more than you do. You could have solved the neurosis question. And here I am . . . a simple citizen . . . by the grace of God having discovered the simple secret that what is, is. I haven't even discovered this. Gertrude Stein has discovered this. I just copy her. No, copy is not right. I got in the same way of living—thinking, with her. Not as an intellectual, but just as a human plant, animal—and this is where you were blind. You moralized and defended sex; taking this out of the total context of life. So you missed life. (There is quiet in the room for several moments. Then Fritz turns to Barbara.) So, your copy of Fritz wasn't so bad. (Gives Barbara a kiss) You did something for me.

Barbara: Thank you, Fritz.

ABOUT THE AUTHOR

DR. FREDERICK S. PERLS was born in Berlin in 1893. He was internationally known as the founder of Gestalt therapy, which is more and more recognized as the most effective innovation in psychiatry since Sigmund Freud. He established the South African Institute for Psychoanalysis in 1935, the New York Institute of Gestalt Therapy in 1952, and the Cleveland Institute for Gestalt Therapy in 1954. For several years he devoted himself to the conduct and recording of seminars and professional workshops in Gestalt therapy. Most recently he turned his attention to the application of the principles of Gestalt therapy to educational practice. He died in Chicago in 1970.